CAMBRIDGE LIBRARY COLLECTION

Books of enduring scholarly value

History

The books reissued in this series include accounts of historical events and movements by eye-witnesses and contemporaries, as well as landmark studies that assembled significant source materials or developed new historiographical methods. The series includes work in social, political and military history on a wide range of periods and regions, giving modern scholars ready access to influential publications of the past.

The Remedy

Thomas Fowell Buxton, M.P. (1786–1845) was a philanthropist who had many connections with the Quaker movement through the family of his wife, who was the sister of Henry Gurney and Elizabeth Fry. He was a passionate opponent of slavery, and campaigned to end it at a time when most British people believed that enough had been done by the abolition of British slave trading in 1807. *The Remedy*, first published in 1840, called on the government to do more to assist African development, so that African chiefs' participation in the trade would be reduced. Many African rulers believed that trade in people was their only economic resource, but Buxton argued that this was false, and that, with training in agriculture and commerce, the available workforce could greatly improve the economy of Africa without slavery. He also advocated greater use of the navy to patrol the coasts of Africa to drive off slavers.

Cambridge University Press has long been a pioneer in the reissuing of out-of-print titles from its own backlist, producing digital reprints of books that are still sought after by scholars and students but could not be reprinted economically using traditional technology. The Cambridge Library Collection extends this activity to a wider range of books which are still of importance to researchers and professionals, either for the source material they contain, or as landmarks in the history of their academic discipline.

Drawing from the world-renowned collections in the Cambridge University Library, and guided by the advice of experts in each subject area, Cambridge University Press is using state-of-the-art scanning machines in its own Printing House to capture the content of each book selected for inclusion. The files are processed to give a consistently clear, crisp image, and the books finished to the high quality standard for which the Press is recognised around the world. The latest print-on-demand technology ensures that the books will remain available indefinitely, and that orders for single or multiple copies can quickly be supplied.

The Cambridge Library Collection will bring back to life books of enduring scholarly value (including out-of-copyright works originally issued by other publishers) across a wide range of disciplines in the humanities and social sciences and in science and technology.

The
Remedy

Being a Sequel to
'The African Slave Trade'

THOMAS FOWELL BUXTON

CAMBRIDGE
UNIVERSITY PRESS

CAMBRIDGE UNIVERSITY PRESS

Cambridge, New York, Melbourne, Madrid, Cape Town, Singapore,
São Paolo, Delhi, Dubai, Tokyo, Mexico City

Published in the United States of America by Cambridge University Press, New York

www.cambridge.org
Information on this title: www.cambridge.org/9781108024327

© in this compilation Cambridge University Press 2010

This edition first published 1840
This digitally printed version 2010

ISBN 978-1-108-02432-7 Paperback

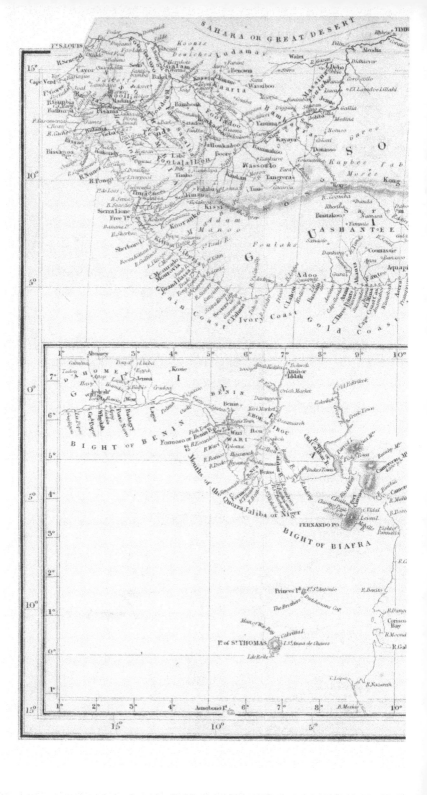

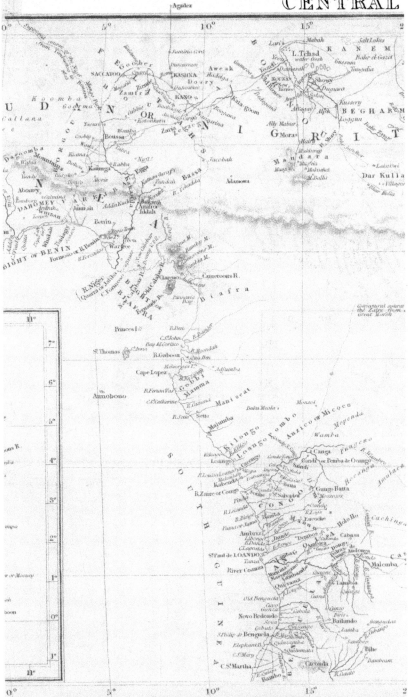

AFRICA

Shendy

Khartoum

Massowa

L.Fittre

Axum

Abu Schum
Kadhama
Kubkabey
Kolbe
Emchokne

Fúli
Bary
Wad Shelterbe

Hurbagt

Abu Haraz

Tamat

SALEY OR BORGOO

Wara

Abu
Shareb

Kagia
Kurbatch
Obeid

SENNAR
OR
Sennar
Ad debibat

Birout

GONDAR

Annal

Troga
Fadow
Fodow
Kil

Abu Haraza

FUNGI

Dar Tunorko

Koldaji
Dreier

El Krebin

ABYSSI

L.Dembia

Gidil

KORDOFAN

Amhara

Gojam

Agot

Dar Marrah

Kollan

Takale

Gebel Geof

Beni
Dembi
Senary of the Nile
Debra
Work
Mekan
Salazze

Misserdal or Oan

Dar Bango or Oan

Dar Fungara

Um Telaho

SHOA&

Bitciah

Guku
Oder

Shaboon

Denka Camp

Suguee

Teguleti

Fertit

Bertat
Mountainous
and Woody

COUNTRY

Copper Mines

Gango
Naria
Gambat
Boshum

Bahr el Abiad or White R.

Kaffa

Bahr el Achla
Tuki Javi

DONGA

Djebel Kumri or Mountains of the Moon

Gingiro

Tribe
and

N I M E A N A I

Equator

Massequejos

R.Quilimanei
Giller
R.Killad
R.Dueyombe
House or Nash R.

Gazith
R.Panyany
Seccone
Arunda

R.Ibargo

Damges

R.Chargo

sange

MILUA
Capital
OR
MOROPOOA

Muiao

KEELWA
R.Quavo
R.Quisimalligh

Dinschirah

QUILOA
Lindy

Mongallos

R.Moryatto or
Monghow
R.Mujais

Varembka

L.Maravi
or Zamba

R.Mozimba

QUERIMB

R.Linuangwe
Quisim

Cazembe Dominions

Capital
Quebule
Chpari

Parsooka

R.Morufura
R.Misanggo

Maxamamba

Quintangunh
R.Ferran Velos

MOZAMBIQUE

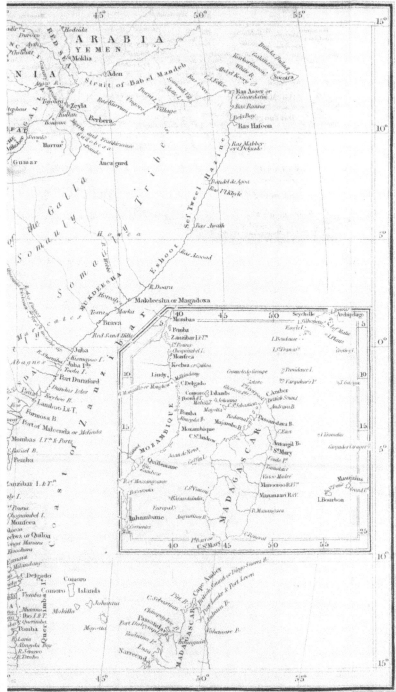

THE REMEDY;

BEING A

SEQUEL

TO THE

AFRICAN SLAVE TRADE.

BY

THOMAS FOWELL BUXTON, Esq.

The desert shall rejoice and blossom as the rose.—Isaiah xxxv. 1.

LONDON:
JOHN MURRAY, ALBEMARLE-STREET.

MDCCCXL.

CONTENTS.

PREFACE.

As the remedy I contemplate is now, for the first
time, published, it is necessary to explain the reason
why it has hitherto been withheld. In the spring of
1838, I stated to several members of the cabinet my
views as to the suppression of the Slave Trade. I
could not reasonably expect, that, in the extreme
pressure of business during the sitting of Parliament,
they would be able to find time to give it the
consideration it required, I therefore prepared for
the press and printed a few copies of my work—describing the horrors of the Slave Trade, and propos-
ing a remedy, for the private use of the members of
the administration, and placed these in their hands
on the day that the session closed. At the latter end
of the year (December 22), after various communi-
cations with Lords Glenelg and Palmerston, I was
officially informed that the Government had resolved

to embrace and to adopt the substance of the plan. A question then arose as to the propriety of printing the whole work. It was thought highly desirable that the public should be put in possession of the facts which showed the extent of the Slave Trade, and the waste of human life which accompanied it. But as a negociation had been commenced with Spain for the cession to Great Britain of the sovereignty of Fernando Po, it was not deemed advisable to give publicity to the intelligence I had obtained as to that island, and the importance I attached to its possession. It was therefore resolved that I should publish the first part, withholding the Remedy till the fate of the negociation was determined ; in consequence of which my first volume was put into circulation in the commencement of the year 1839.

The negociation has not, I regret to say, been as yet brought to an issue ; but it is in that state, that a definitive answer must speedily be received, and I am assured that there is no occasion for any further delay.

There is another point upon which I wish to make myself clearly intelligible. Some of my most valuable associates have given me a friendly intimation that they " hold themselves wholly distinct from any measure the Government may adopt with respect to

the defence of the Colonies, or the suppression of the
Slave Trade by armed force; and that they are not
to be considered responsible for the recommendations
that any member of our committee may make, in
connexion with such measures." This is a protest
against those passages in my Remedy in which I
advise that our squadron may for the present be rendered more efficient, and that our settlements should
be protected by the British Government. I entirely
feel, that the gentlemen who have made the protest
cannot be considered as parties to this recommendation. It was a suggestion of my own—it was offered
to Government before they had seen it—and Government will take its own course upon the subject. In
my book I propose two distinct courses; and I couple
them together in the same work, because the arguments
employed bear upon each of these separate questions.
In other words, I apply to the Government to do one
thing for the suppression of the Slave Trade, viz. to
strengthen our squadron; and I apply to individuals
to join me in measures having the same object, but of
a character totally different. Such, for example, as
an attempt to elevate the mind of the people of
Africa, and to call forth the capabilities of her soil.

I have no wish to disguise my sentiments about
armed force. I deprecate, as much as any man, re-
sorting to violence and war. These are against the

whole tenor of my views. It will be admitted, I think, that I have laboured hard in this book to show, that our great error has been, that we have depended far too much upon physical force. It is, however, the duty of our Government to see that the peace of our settlements be preserved. The natives whom we induce to engage in agriculture must not be exposed to the irruption of a savage banditti, instigated by some miscreant from Europe, whose vessel waits upon the shore for a human cargo. Nor must our runaway sailors repeat in Africa the atrocities which have been practised in New Zealand. Again and again the Foulah tribes said to the missionaries on the river Gambia, " Give us security, and we will gladly till the land and pasture the cattle in your neighbourhood." There were no means of thus protecting them, and hence an experiment, founded on admirable principles, failed. But when I ask for an effectual police force, I ask for that only. I do not desire the employment of such a military force as might be perverted into the means of war and conquest. I want only, that the man engaged in lawful and innocent employment in Africa, should have the same protection as an agricultural labourer or a mechanic receives in England; and that there, as well as here, the murderer and man-stealer may be arrested and punished.

It is possible that in these views I may be mistaken; and that the gentlemen to whom I allude may wholly differ from me. But there is no reason because they do so, avowing their dissent, that they should abstain from joining me in the task of delivering Africa from the Slave Trade by the means of her own mind, and her own resources, developed and cultivated. In this object we heartily agree; and for its accomplishment we may heartily unite. I number amongst my coadjutors very many of the Society of Friends; but I prize too highly the disinterested and unflinching zeal with which that body pursues the objects which it approves, to be content to lose any individual of the number, especially through a misapprehension; and it is for the purpose of averting this, that I have thought it necessary to enter into this explanation.

I have already described the state of Africa. It will on all hands be said that there are great, if not invincible, difficulties to the application of a remedy. This is but too true. There is only one consideration strong enough to prompt us to grapple with these difficulties, namely, a just apprehension of her miseries. I pray my readers not to shrink from the task of sedulously studying the facts collected in this book. In the case of Africa, I fear hardly anything

so much as the indulgence of excessive tenderness
of feeling. If the benevolent and religious portion
of the public choose to content themselves with the
general and superficial conviction, that there is no
doubt a great mass of misery in Africa, but refuse to
sift and scrutinize each circumstance of horror,
pleading the susceptibility of their nerves as an apology to themselves for shutting their eyes and closing
their ears to such revolting details ; then the best
hope for Africa—perhaps the only hope—vanishes
away. That resolute, unflinching, untiring deter-
mination which is necessary, in order to surmount
the difficulties which lie in the way of her deliverance, requires not only that the understanding should
be convinced, but that the heart should be moved.
Our feelings will be far too tame for the occasion,
unless we can, in pity to Africa, summon courage
enough to face, and to study, the horrors of the Slave
Trade, and the abominations which there grow out of
a dark and bloody superstition.

INTRODUCTION.

It has been no very difficult task to collect materials for a description of the varied and intense miseries with which Africa is afflicted. Every person who visits that country,—whether his motive be the pursuit of traffic or the gratification of curiosity, the prosecution of geographical science or of missionary labour,—brings back a copious collection of details calculated to excite pity, disgust, and horror.

Happy would it be if it were as easy to point out the remedy, as to explore the disease.

To this task I now address myself, difficult though it be, from various causes—from the magnitude of the evil—from the vast and complicated interests involved—and from the comparative scantiness of our information. For, while the miseries of Africa are such as meet the eye of the most casual traveller,—while her crimes and woes are such as no one can overlook ;— the sources from whence we must hope for the remedy lie much deeper and far more hidden from our view. We know so little really of the interior of Africa,— her geography, her history, her soil, climate, and productions,—so little of the true condition and capa-

bilities of her inhabitants, that (having collected all
the information within my reach) it is with very great
diffidence I venture to put forth what appear to me,
to be the principles which must rescue her, and the
steps which we, as a nation, and as individuals,
are called upon to take, to carry those principles into
operation.

In one respect I apprehend no liability to error.
With all confidence we may affirm, that nothing permanent will be effected, unless *we raise the native
mind.* It is possible to conceive such an application
of force, as shall blockade the whole coast, and sweep
away every slaver: but should that effort relax, the
trade in man would revive. Compulsion, so long as
it lasts, may restrain the act, but it will not eradicate
the motive. The African will not have ceased to
desire, and vehemently to crave, the spirits, the
ammunition, and the articles of finery and commerce
which Europe alone can supply : and these he can obtain by the Slave Trade, and by the Slave Trade only,
while he remains what he is. The pursuit of man,
therefore, is to him not a matter of choice and selection, but of necessity, and after any interval of con-
strained abstinence he will revert to it as the business
of his life.

But, when the African nations shall emerge from
their present state of darkness and debasement, they
will require no arguments from us, to convince them
of the monstrous impolicy of the Slave Trade. They
will not be content to see their remaining territories

a wilderness, themselves in penury, their villages
exposed day after day to havoc and conflagration, their
children kidnapped and slaughtered,—and all for the
purpose of gaining a paltry supply of the most inferior and pernicious articles of Europe. They will
perceive, that their effective strength may be applied
to other, and more lucrative purposes : and as their
intellect advances, it is not too much to hope that
their morals will improve, and that they will awaken
to the enormous wickedness, as well as folly, of this
cruel system. " Europe, therefore," (to use the words
of one of the most distinguished of African travellers,*) "will have done little for the Blacks, if the
abolition of the Atlantic Slave Trade is not followed
up by some wise and grand plan for the civilization
of the continent. None presents a fairer prospect
than the education of the sons of Africa in their own
country, and by their own countrymen previously
educated by Europeans."

We may assume, and with almost equal confidence, that Africa can never be delivered, till we
have called forth the rich productiveness of her soil.
She derives, it must be confessed, some pecuniary
advantage from the Slave Trade : happily, however,
it is the smallest possible amount of revenue, at
the largest possible amount of cost. The strength
of our case, and the foundation of our hope, lie in
the assurance;—I am tempted rather to call it, the
indisputable certainty,—that the soil will yield a far

* Burckhardt, p. 344.

more generous return.   Grant that the chieftains
sell every year 250,000 of the inhabitants, and that into
their hands £4 per head is honestly paid. (This is not
the fact, however, for they are often defrauded altogether, and are always cheated by receiving merchandise of the most inferior description.) But let us
suppose that they get the value of one million of
money : we have, from this sum, to deduct, first, the
cost of maintaining their armies intended for the
Slave Trade : then of the reprisals which are made
upon themselves, and the consequent ravage of their
land and destruction of their property : thirdly, the
material items of arms, ammunition, and ardent
spirits, which form one-third of the whole of the
goods imported into Central Africa, and the greater
part of which are consumed in their horrid slave-
hunts :*—to say nothing of any indirect loss, such
as millions of fertile acres being left a desert;
—nothing of perils encountered and torments en-
dured ;—making no other abatement than the three
sources of direct and unavoidable expense which I
have named,—the million will have melted away
to a very slender sum.   Call the clear profit, for
argument's sake, £300,000 ;—and is £300,000 all
that can be reaped from so extensive a portion of the

* I remember it was given in evidence before a Parliamentary
Committee, that an African chief thus concisely stated his mercantile views :—" We want three things, viz. powder, ball, and
brandy ; and we have three things to sell, viz. men, women, and
children. "

globe, inferior to none other in native wealth? Her
fisheries, separately taken, would yield more; or her
mines, or her timber, or her drugs, her indigo, or her
sugar, or her cotton.

I am then stedfast in my belief, that the capabilities of Africa would furnish full compensation to
that country for the loss of the Slave Trade. It may
sound visionary at the present time, but I expect that
at some future, and not very distant day, it will
appear, that for every pound she now receives from
the export of her people, a hundred pounds' worth
of produce, either for home consumption or foreign
commerce, will be raised from the fertility of her
soil.

It is something to know that there is a natural and
an infallible remedy for the distractions of Africa,
and that the remedy is within reach, were there but
the sagacity to use it. It is another question, how
we shall cause that remedy to be applied, and how
we shall make manifest to the clouded perceptions of
her people, the false economy of selling her effective
strength, while her plains remain a desert, instead
of employing that strength in transforming that
desert into a fruitful and smiling land. Capabilities are nothing to the unreflecting mind of the
savage : he wants something present and tan-
gible.

How then shall we undeceive her chiefs, and convince them, that it is for their interest that the Slave
Trade should cease? This we *must* do for Africa:

we must elevate the minds of her people, and call forth the capabilities of her soil.

Bearing in mind, that every effort we make must be intended, either directly or remotely, to effect one, or other, or both of these objects, I now proceed to a detail of the remedial measures which it seems necessary to adopt.

CHAPTER I.

The first thing to be done, is to throw all possible impediments in the way of the Slave Trade, and to make it both more precarious and less profitable than it is at present.

In order to do this, *our squadron must be rendered more efficient;* and this it is supposed may be accomplished—

1st. By concentrating on the coast of Africa the whole force employed in this particular service. It has been our practice hitherto to distribute a few ships along the African coast, while others cruise near South America and the West Indies. The former, though they have failed in suppressing the trade, have at all events done something towards the annoyance of the trader. The latter, with equal zeal, and a much larger force, have done little or nothing towards this object. On the average of the last four years to which the accounts extend, viz., 1834-5-6 and 7, we have had on the West Indian and South American stations 42 vessels of war; on the African station, 14. By the former there have been taken and adjudicated, in four years, 34 slavers; by the smaller squadron, 97.

I am not so ignorant as to infer that the Admi-

2 THETHE REMEDY.

ralty were in error in this distribution of their disposable force. I well know that other objects than the
suppression of the Slave Trade demanded attention :
as little do I presume to cast any reflection upon
the naval officers in command. But from these facts I
conceive I am entitled to draw the conclusion, that,
as far as the Slave Trade is concerned, little or no
benefit has been derived from the force stationed in
the neighbourhood of Cuba and Brazil.

2dly. The efficiency of our squadron may be improved by an actual increase of the force.

I am aware that some gentlemen, seeing that all
our past naval efforts have failed, are in favour of
withdrawing our whole force, and of relying exclusively on other means; but it appears to me, that in
order to try these other means with the most advantage, it is needful, for a time, to retain our force on
the coast of Africa.

If at the moment when we are beginning to
encourage agricultural industry, and to give an impulse to the minds of her people, our navy were to
abandon the coast, there can be no doubt that it
would be a signal to the chiefs of the country (still
ignorant of the resources of their soil, and still supposing that the Slave Trade alone can supply them
with the luxuries of Europe) to prosecute their horrid
traffic with even more than their usual energy.
They would avail themselves of the removal of the
only check which they have hitherto felt, and at the
very moment when our last ship departed from the

coast, Africa would present a scene of conflagration, massacre, and convulsion, such as even Africa has never before witnessed.

Can it be imagined that agriculture could thrive or the voice of the teacher receive attention, or the arts of peace take root, at such a moment? Having persevered so long and so unprofitably in the attempt to suppress the traffic by force, it would be a poor mode of repairing our error, to dismiss that force just at the time when we most required tranquillity, and when anything likely to give a new impulse to the Slave Trade would be peculiarly unseasonable.

It would appear to be a wiser policy to augment our force, and thus to multiply the risks, while we reduce the profits of the trade. We should try, if it were only for a given period, the full effect of what can be done by our maritime strength: instead of doling out, year by year, a force inadequate to our object, we should at this juncture strike a telling blow, so that the African, while measuring the advantages of that system which we wish him to abandon, against that which we desire to see adopted, may feel in its greatest force the weight of those hazards and discouragements which the British navy can interpose.

3dly. We may increase the efficiency of our squadron by the employment of steamers as part of the proposed reinforcement. I am, it must be confessed, but ill qualified to offer an opinion on a matter which comes rather within the province of naval officers. I can only say, that amongst the many persons conversant with the coast of Africa, and with the Slave Trade, from whom I have sought information, I have not met with an individual who has not urged that steamers might be employed with great advantage. It is not only, that they would be able to explore rivers and harbours, which other vessels cannot enter, but that in latitudes where frequent calms prevail, they might often come up with slavers, which have hitherto escaped our cruisers. We know too well, that with his slaves safely on board, and his vessel fairly at sea, it is not often that the slave trader is captured. " Once outside in my trim vessel, you may catch me if you can,"* is, unhappily, something more than an empty vaunt. In the proposed employment of steamers, to search the mouths of rivers, one precaution is indispensable. They must be manned by persons who can bear the climate to which they will be exposed. Admiral Elliott, now commanding on this station, objects to exploring the rivers, on account of the loss of life which invariably follows among British seamen : he recommends the enlistment of black seamen for this service, and the purchase of small armed steamers to be employed exclusively in river navigation.

I may as well say here, once for all, that, in all our African undertakings, I look to the employment (except in a very few cases) of the negro and coloured race, and that I have reason to believe that

* Vide page 164.

well qualified agents of that description may be procured without difficulty.

I proceed now to the suggestion of a second preparatory measure.

*Treaties should be formed with native powers in
Africa*—they receiving certain advantages, propor-
tioned to the assistance they afford in the prosecution
of our objects, and engaging on their side, to put down
the Slave Trade. I do not mean to say, that this is
all that ought to be contemplated in these treaties.
To give facilities for commerce and agricultural settlements will be a subject of consideration hereafter.
All I urge at this point of the argument, is, that we
should do our utmost to obtain the cordial co-operation of the natives in the suppression of their detestable
traffic.

I am aware that a formidable objection to this proposition will present itself to many of my readers.
It will be said, that it is visionary to suppose that these
barbarian chieftains can be induced, except by force
of arms, to connect themselves with us,—to lend us
their aid in extinguishing their only trade,—to enter
into peaceable commerce with us; and, yet more,
to admit us, as friends, into their dominions, and
voluntarily to grant us such an extent of territory
and of privileges, as shall enable us to plant settlements among them.

I trust, however, that in this case, we are to be
guided, not by preconceived opinions, but by facts
gathered from experience. The truth is, and on this

my hopes are built, that the natives, so far from shunning intercourse with us, and rejecting our overtures for peace and commerce, have been, in almost every case, eager and importunate that we should settle among them. If further progress has not been made, it is ourselves who have been to blame. I find abundant instances in which they have declared their willingness and ability to suppress the Slave Trade, and in which they have offered to grant every facility for commerce, —to cede territory,—and, in not a few cases, to put themselves under our dominion. I find even treaties to this effect, formed between British officers and native chiefs. But I can seldom find that these invitations to amity and commerce have been encouraged, or that these treaties have been ratified by the Home Government.

I grant that this anxiety on the part of the negroes to hold communication with us, is one of the most unexpected, as it is one of the most encouraging features of the whole case. It would have been far from strange if the disposition of African potentates had been adverse to a connexion with us. They have had but little reason to think favourably of European intentions, or to feel any great reverence for those who bear the name of Christians. If they are otherwise than distrustful of us, it must arise from their drawing a distinction between the course we pursue in Africa, and that taken by other civilised nations; and from their having learnt by experience duly to appreciate the nature of our settlements at

Sierra Leone and elsewhere ; or else from a deeper
sense than we give them credit for, of their own forlorn
and disastrous condition, and a conviction that they
would be likely to improve it by intercourse with us.
It may be, that they loathe their present evils further
than we know, and, feeling impotent to rise out of
their distresses by their own vigour, hope for deliverance through our instrumentality. But we must reason
on facts as we find them ; and I believe that they bear
me out in stating, that there exists throughout the
whole space, from Senegambia to Benin, a marked
confidence in the British ; and not only a readiness, but
an anxiety, to have us for their neighbours, and to
enter into amicable relations with us. I need not say
how much depends upon the truth or fallacy of this
statement. If it be true, many of the most formidable difficulties in our way are removed, and there
will be, at least, an admitted possibility of a league
between England and Africa,—for the suppression of
the Slave Trade,—for the spread of commerce,—and
for the development of those vast resources which are
buried in the African soil. This, then, I shall endeavour to prove ; but as there is an exception to this
facility of intercourse, I will state it at once.

I suspect it will be very difficult to gain the concurrence of the chiefs on the coast : these, in the words
of a gentleman who has spent many years in studying
the geography of Africa, and the character of its inhabitants, are " a rabble of petty chiefs, the most ignorant and rude, and the greatest vagabonds on earth."

They have been rendered habitual drunkards by the spirits which Slave Ships supply. As slave-factors, they have been steeled against all compassion and all sympathy with human suffering; and no better influence has been exercised over them, than that derived from intercourse with the dregs of Europe. Besides, they obtain a two-fold advantage from the Slave Trade. The goods they obtain from Europeans give a considerable profit when sold to the natives, while the slaves, received by them in return for those goods, yield a profit still more considerable, when sold to the slave-captain.

We must then expect great opposition from the chiefs on the coast. It appears, indeed, from the journals of all travellers in Africa, that every impediment has been thrown in their way, in order to prevent their proceeding to the interior of the country. It is, however, some consolation to learn from recent travellers, that the power of these chiefs has been greatly exaggerated.

But whatever difficulties we may have to encounter with the chiefs on the coast, (and I confess that, viewing their character, and the insalubrity of the climate near the sea, and at the mouths of rivers, I apprehend that they will be far from light,) there is good reason to believe that we shall find a much better disposition on the part of the Sultans and sovereigns of the interior, to receive, to treat, and to trade with us. I shall endeavour to show, first, that with respect to the two most powerful potentates of Central Africa, the Sheikh of Bornou, and the Sultan of the Felatahs, there is some reason for supposing that we need not despair of their co-operation.

Major Denham, in speaking of the Slave Trade at Bornou, says :—" I think I may say, that neither the Sheikh himself, nor the Bornou people, carry on the traffic without feelings of disgust, which even habit cannot conquer. Of the existence of a foreign Slave Trade, or one which consigns these unfortunates to Christian masters, they are not generally aware at Bornou ; and so contrary to the tenets of his religion, (Mahometanism,) of which he is a strict observer, would be such a system of barter, that one may easily conclude the Sheikh of Bornou would be willing to assist, with all the power he possesses, in any plan which might have for its object the putting a final stop to a commerce of this nature.

" The eagerness with which all classes of people listened to our proposals for establishing a frequent communication by means of European merchants, and the protection promised by the Sheikh to such as should arrive within the sphere of his influence, particularly if they were English, excites an anxious hope that some measures will be adopted for directing the labours of a population of millions, to something more congenial to the humanity and the philanthropy of the age we live in, than the practice of a system of predatory warfare, which has chiefly for its object the procuring of slaves, as the readiest and most valuable property to trade with.

" Every probability is against such a barter being preferred by the African black. Let the words of the Sheikh himself, addressed to us, in the hearing of his people, speak the sentiments that have already found a place in his bosom :—'You say true, we are all sons of one father! You say, also, that the sons of Adam should not sell one another, and you know everything! God has given you all great talents, but what are we to do? The Arabs who come here will have nothing else but slaves : why don't you send us your merchants? You know us now, and let them bring their women with them, and live amongst us, and teach us what you talk to me about so often, to build houses, and boats, and make rockets.' "

He adds, " Wherever El Kenemy, the sultan of Bornou, has power, Europeans, and particularly Englishmen, will be hospitably and kindly received. Although harassed by the constant wars in which he has been engaged, yet has not the Sheikh been unmindful of the benefits which an extended commerce would confer upon his people, nor of the importance of improving their moral condition, by exciting a desire to acquire, by industry and trade, more permanent and certain advantages than are to be obtained by a system of plunder and destructive warfare. Arab or Moorish merchants, the only ones who have hitherto ventured amongst them, are encouraged and treated with great liberality.

"It was with feelings of the highest satisfaction that I listened to some of the most respectable of the merchants, when they declared, that were any other system of trading adopted, they would gladly embrace it, in preference to dealing in slaves."

Denham makes these observations in 1824; in 1830, Richard Lander says, he learnt that the Sheikh of Bornou had prohibited the carrying of slaves any farther to the westward (that is, towards the coast) than Wawa, a town on the borders of his empire; and it is not unworthy of notice, that when Lander was at this place a few years before, the chief of Wawa said to him, "Tell your countrymen that they have my permission to come here and build a town, and trade up and down the Quorra" (the Niger).

Captain Clapperton visited Bello, the powerful sultan of the Felatahs, in 1823, at Sackatoo. Their conversation often turned on the Slave Trade, which Clapperton urged the sultan to discontinue. Bello asked the captain, if the king of England would send him a consul, and a physician, to reside in Soudan, and merchants to trade with his people? Clapperton said he had no doubt his wishes would be gratified, provided he would suppress the Slave Trade. The Sultan replied, "I will give the king of England a place on the coast to build a town." On another occasion, he assured Clapperton that he was able to put an effectual stop to the Slave Trade; and ex-

pressed, with much earnestness of manner, his anxi
ety to enter into permanent relations of trade and
friendship with England. At the close of Clapperton's visit, Bello gave him a letter to the king of
England, to the same purport as the conversation
which had taken place between them. These offers
on the part of the Sultan of the Felatahs must be
held to be of great importance. He is the chief of
a warlike, enterprising people, who have extended
their sway over many of the nations and tribes around
them; and who, from the testimony of recent travellers, are actively employed in carrying on war
with their neighbours to supply the demands of the
Slave Trade. It appears that Captain Clapperton
met with an ungracious reception from Sultan Bello,
in his last visit to Sackatoo in 1826; but this is
accounted for by the Sultan's having discovered
that Clapperton was on his way to visit his rival,
the Sheik of Bornou, with whom he was then at
war, and by the jealousy of the Arab merchants and
slave-dealers, who had carefully instilled into his
mind, of suspicions as to the intentions of Great Britain. I am not aware that anything has been done to
counteract this impression; but it would not be difficult to disabuse the mind of Bello, who would, no
doubt, be induced by a few presents, to afford his
countenance and protection to British trade, by which
Houssa would be so greatly benefited.

I will now proceed to prove, that there likewise
exists on the part of the chiefs of less powerful tribes a

disposition to enter into friendly relations with us. I give a single illustration :—In a despatch from Acting Governor Grant, dated Sierra Leone, 28th February, 1821, I find that "an application had been made to Governor Macarthy by the king of the Foulahs, a very powerful prince in the interior, expressing a desire to have an officer sent up to Teemboo, the capital of his territories; and having myself," he says, "received a very friendly letter from the king, I was induced, in conformity with Governor Macarthy's intentions, to despatch Mr. O'Beirn, assistant-surgeon to the forces, on that service. The influence of the Foulah nation, extending from the branches of the Sierra Leone River to the banks of the Niger, and communicating with the principal countries of the interior, renders a friendly connexion with that country of much importance to our commercial interests; and it is with much satisfaction I have to report the good effect of Mr. O'Beirn's exertions; which are already felt here, in the increased supply of ivory, gold, and cattle, brought by the Foulahs to our different factories situate on this river. Mr. O'Beirn is merely accompanied by a few people of colour to carry his luggage and presents, the expense of which will be trifling." He was received in the most friendly manner possible at Teemboo, the capital of the Foulah nation, by the king, Almami Abdool Kaddree.

The following is an extract from Mr. O'Beirn's Journal :—" I never saw more joy and complacency in any countenance, than his expressed, on my being introduced to him, and I have seldom in my life experienced such a kind and warm reception." The chiefs were assembled to hear his explanation of the objects of his mission : he explained to them the great advantage they would derive from carrying on a trade with the colony, and how much superior such a trade would be to the traffic in slaves; and told them, what England had done to put an end to it, and to give freedom to their countrymen.

"Almami replied, that he had for many years wished for a communication to be opened between Sierra Leone and his country, Foota Jalloo, and that it should continue free and uninterrupted to the latest day; adding, that it was not his fault, or it would have been effected years before. He likewise re-- marked, with respect to what I had said of the Slave Trade, it was his opinion that it would be given up ere long; that is, sending them for sale to the coast, and that he was fully convinced he would be brought to account in the next world for disposing of his fellow-creatures in that way; but hoped, at the same time, God would accept the excuse of the impossibility that formerly existed of procuring the necessaries of life in such abundance, or resisting the inducements held out, at that time, by the white people that came to purchase them."

I do not wish to impose upon my readers the monotonous task of travelling through a variety of such treaties which these chieftains have made, or have offered to make, with the British Government: these will be given in the Appendix;* and I apprehend that those who take the trouble of examining them will find, that there is no unwillingness on their part to grant any reasonable quantity of land,—any powers however extensive,—and any conditions for the suppression of the Slave Trade, that we may think proper to propose; and that all this may be obtained for the trifling consideration of a few dollars, or a few pieces of baft. I am ready to admit that little benefit has hitherto resulted from these negociations, but this does not arise from any faithlessness on the part of the natives in the fulfilment of their engagements; on the contrary, I may quote the unexceptionable authority of Mr. Bandinel, of the Foreign Office, for the fact, that "compacts for the suppression of the Slave Trade have been concluded with the chiefs of several native states, and that those treaties have been faithfully maintained by the native sovereigns." Mr. Rendall, late Governor of the Gambia, also says:—" With respect to the general conduct of the chiefs, I am not aware of our having any just cause to complain of a breach of confidence being committed in the treaties heretofore made with them, nor do I think there is any just cause to fear that they are now more likely to forfeit their words and honour, particularly in cases where their interests are studiously considered."

The reason why greater advantage has not been

* Vide Appendix A.

derived from co-operation with these powers, is, as I have before intimated, that the British Government has discountenanced almost all efforts in that direction. "It has never," says Mr. H. Macaulay, Commissary Judge of Sierra Leone, in his evidence before the Aborigines Committee, in 1837, "been the policy of our government from the first, while it was in the hands of the company, nor since it has been transferred to the crown, to extend our territory in any way. Even when General Turner and Sir Neil Campbell were governors in former years, and acquired by treaty, and other just means, territory in the neighbourhood, and paid for it, the government ordered us to give it back. They would not allow us to take possession of it and occupy it as a British territory. And though, in my opinion, it would be desirable to extend our territory as our population increases so much, yet it has not been done." To the question—"Do you think it would be expedient or just to take possession of the territory of these people without their consent?" He answers, "Certainly not; but we are such good neighbours, and they have such perfect confidence in us, that I think there would be no difficulty in acquiring territory by treaty." "Have you found any difficulty in preserving relations of amity with the surrounding natives?"—"None whatever."

It appears to me well worth while to adopt an entirely new line of policy, and to establish, to the utmost extent possible, a confederacy with the chiefs, from the Gambia on the West, to Begharmi on the East; and from the Desert on the North, to the Gulf of Guinea on the South.

Thus, I have suggested two distinct kinds of preparatory measures.

1st. An augmentation of the naval force employed in the suppression of the Slave Trade, and the concentration of that force on the coast of Africa, thus forming a chain of vessels from Gambia to Angola.

2ndly. A corresponding chain of treaties with native powers in the interior, pledging them to act in concert with us; to suppress the Slave Trade in their own territory; to prevent slaves from being carried through their dominions, and, at the same time, to afford all needful facility and protection for the transport of legitimate merchandise. Thus, by creating obstacles which have not heretofore existed, in the conveyance of negroes to the coast, and by increasing the hazard of capture after embarkation, I cannot but anticipate that we shall greatly increase the costs and multiply the risks of the Slave Trade.

If I am asked, whether I expect thus to effect its total abolition, I answer distinctly, No :—such measures may reduce, or even suspend, but they cannot eradicate the evil. If we succeed in establishing a blockade of the coast, together with a confederacy on shore, and proceed no further, it will still be doubtful, as it has been in our former operations, whether more of good or of evil will be effected ;— good, by the degree of restraint imposed on the traffic,

C

or evil, by rendering what remains concealed and contraband ; and when I recur to the fearful aggravation of the sufferings of the slaves, which has already arisen from this cause, I am almost disposed to think that it were better to do nothing than to do only this.

I propose the two measures I have just named, not as a remedy, but as an expedient necessary for a time, in order that the real remedy may be applied in the most effectual manner. For a time, the dangers and difficulties of the slave-trader must be increased, in order that the demand for slaves on the coast may be reduced in the interval that must necessarily elapse before a total suppression can be effected. There was a time, during the last war, when our cruisers were so numerous in the African seas, that it was difficult for a slaver to escape; and it was then observed that the chiefs betook themselves to agriculture and trade.

The greater the impediments that are thrown in the way of obtaining supplies through the accustomed channels, the stronger becomes the inducement to procure them in another and better mode; and thus, the diminution of the Slave Trade will operate as an encouragement to industry, and a stimulus to commerce. And the evil being thus temporarily held in check, time and space, so to speak, will be given for the effectual operation of the remedy.

CHAPTER II.

COMMERCE AND CULTIVATION.

"It was not possible for me to behold the fertility of the soil, the vast herds of cattle, proper both for labour and food, and a variety of other circumstances favourable to colonization and agriculture, and reflect withal on the means which presented themselves of a vast inland navigation, without lamenting that a country so abundantly gifted and honoured by nature, should remain in its present savage and neglected state."—PARK.

"The commercial intercourse of Africa opens an inexhaustible source of wealth to the manufacturing interests of Great Britain—to all which the Slave Trade is a physical obstruction."—GUSTAVUS VASA. *Letter to Lord Hawkesbury.* 1788.

But what is the true remedy ? It cannot be too deeply engraven upon the minds of British statesmen, that it is beyond our power to rescue Africa, if the burthen is to fall wholly and permanently on ourselves. It is not the partial aid, lent by a distant nation, but the natural and healthy exercise of her own energies, which will ensure success. We cannot *create* a remedy; but, if it be true that this remedy already exists, and that nothing is wanting but its right application—if Africa possesses within herself vast, though as yet undeveloped, resources,—we may be competent to achieve the much less onerous task of calling forth her powers,

c 2

and enabling her to stand alone, relying upon the strength of her own native sinews. The work will be done, when her population shall be sufficiently enlightened to arrive at the conviction, (grounded on what their eyes see, and their hands handle,) that the wealth readily to be obtained from peaceful industry, surpasses the slender and precarious profits of rapine.

Our system hitherto has been to obtain the co-operation of European powers, while we have paid very little attention to what might be done in Africa itself, for the suppression of the Slave Trade. Our efforts in that direction have been few, faint, and limited to isolated spots, and those by no means well chosen. To me it appears that the converse of this policy would have offered greater probabilities of success; that, while no reasonable expectations can be entertained of overturning this gigantic evil through the agency and with the concurrence of the civilised world, there is a well-founded hope, amounting almost to a certainty, that this object may be attained through the medium and with the concurrence of Africa herself. If, instead of our expensive and fruitless negotiations with Portugal, we had been, during the last twenty years, engaged in extending our intercourse with the nations of Africa, unfolding to them the capabilities of her soil, and the inexhaustible store of wealth which human labour might derive from its cultivation, and convincing them that the Slave Trade alone debars them from enjoying a vastly more affluent supply of our valuable commodities, and if we had leagued ourselves with them to suppress that baneful traffic, which is their enemy even more than it is ours, there is reason to believe that Africa would not have been what Africa is, in spite of all our exertions,—one universal den of desolation, misery, and crime.

Why do I despair of winning the hearty co-operation of those European powers who now encourage or connive at the Slave Trade? I answer, because we have no sufficient bribe to offer. The secret of their resistance is the 180 per cent. profit which attaches to the Slave Trade. This is a temptation which we cannot outbid. It has been, and it will be, the source of their persevering disregard of the claims of humanity, and of their contempt for the engagements, however solemn, which they have contracted with us.

But why do I entertain a confident persuasion that we may obtain the cordial concurrence of the African powers? Because the Slave Trade is not their gain, but their loss. It is their ruin, because it is capable of demonstration, that, but for the Slave Trade, the other trade of Africa would be increased fifty or a hundred-fold. Because central Africa now receives in exchange for all her exports, both of people and productions, less than half a million of imports, one-half of which may be goods of the worst description, and a third made up of arms and ammunition. What a wretched return is this, for the productions of so

vast, so fertile, so magnificent a territory! Take
the case of central Africa; the insignificance of our
trade with it is forcibly exhibited by contrasting the
whole return from thence, with some single article of
no great moment which enters Great Britain. The
feathers received at Liverpool from Ireland reach an
amount exceeding all the productions of central
Africa; the eggs from France and Ireland exceed
one-half of it; while the value of pigs from Ireland
into the port of Liverpool is three times as great as
the whole trade of Great Britain in the productions of
the soil of central Africa.* What an exhibition does
this give of the ruin which the Slave Trade entails
on Africa! Can it be doubted that, with the extinction of that blight, there would arise up a commerce
which would pour into Africa European articles of
a vastly superior quality, and to a vastly superior
amount?

If it be true that Africa would be enriched, and
that her population would enjoy, in multiplied abundance, those commodities, for the acquisition of which
she now incurs such intense misery, the one needful

	£.
* Eggs, total amount unknown, but into London, Liverpool, and Glasgow, from France and Ireland alone	275,000
Feathers from Ireland to Liverpool (Porter's "Progress of Nation," p. 83) . .	500,000
Pigs from Ireland to Liverpool (Porter, Ibid.)	1,488,555
Total imports, productions of the soil of Central Africa (Porter's Tables, Supplement, No. 5)	456,014

thing, in order to induce them to unite with us in repressing the Slave Trade, is, to convince them that they will gain by selling the productive labour of the people, instead of the people themselves.

My first object, then, is to show that Africa possesses within herself the means of obtaining, by fair trade, a greater quantity of our goods than she now receives from the Slave Trade ; and, secondly, to point out how this truth may be made plain to the African nations. I have further to prove, that Great Britain, and other countries (for the argument applies as much to them as to us), have an interest in the question only inferior to that of Africa, and that if we cannot be persuaded to suppress the Slave Trade for the fear of God, or in pity to man, it ought to be done for the lucre of gain.

The importance of Africa, as a vast field of European commerce, though it has been frequently adverted to, and its advantages distinctly pointed out by those who have visited that part of the world, has not hitherto sufficiently engaged public attention, or led to any great practical results. It is, perhaps, not difficult to account for the apathy which has been manifested on this subject—Africa has a bad name ; its climate is represented, and not altogether unjustly, as pestilential, and destructive of European life ; its population as barbarous and ignorant, indolent and cruel—more addicted to predatory warfare than to the arts of peace ; and its interior as totally inaccessible to European enterprise. With the exception of

a few spots, such as Sierra Leone, the Gambia, the
Senegal, &c., its immensely extended line of coast is
open to the ravages and demoralization of the Slave
Trade, and the devastating incursions of pirates. The
difficulties connected with the establishment of a legitimate commerce with Africa may be traced principally to these circumstances; and could they be removed, by the removal of their cause, the obstacles
arising from climate—the supposed character of its
people—and the difficulty of access to the interior,
would be easily overcome.

Legitimate commerce would put down the Slave
Trade, by demonstrating the superior value of man
as a labourer on the soil, to man as an object of
merchandise; and if conducted on wise and equitable principles, might be the precursor, or rather
the attendant, of civilisation, peace, and Christianity,
to the unenlightened, warlike, and heathen tribes who
now so fearfully prey on each other, to supply the
slave-markets of the New World. In this view of
the subject, the merchant, the philanthropist, the
patriot, and the Christian, may unite; and should
the Government of this country lend its powerful influence in organising a commercial system of just,
liberal, and comprehensive principles—guarding the
rights of the native on the one hand, and securing protection to the honest trader on the other,—a blow
would be struck at the nefarious traffic in human
beings, from which it could not recover; and the
richest blessings would be conferred on Africa, so

long desolated and degraded by its intercourse with the basest and most iniquitous part of mankind.

The present condition of Africa in relation to commerce is deplorable.

The whole amount of goods exported direct from Great Britain to all Africa is considerably within one million sterling.

In the year 1835, the declared value of British and Irish produce and manufactures exported to the whole of Africa was £917,726.

Central Africa possesses within itself everything from which commerce springs. No country in the world has nobler rivers, or more fertile soil ; and it contains a population of fifty millions.

This country, which ought to be amongst the chief of our customers, takes from us only to the value of £312,938 of our manufactures, £101,104* of which are made up of the value of arms and ammunition, and lead and shot.

I must request the reader to fix his attention on these facts; they present a dreadful picture of the moral prostration of Africa,—of the power of the Slave Trade in withering all healthy commerce,—of the atrocious means resorted to, in order to maintain and perpetuate its horrors,—and of the very slender sum which can be put down as expended in fair and honest trading.

The declared value of British and Irish produce

* Parliamentary Returns for 1837.

and manufactures, exported in 1837, was, according
to parliamentary returns—

To Asia	£4,639,736
America . . .	15,496,552
Australia . . .	921,568
Hayti . . .	171,050
Central Africa . .	312,938

Deducting from this last sum the value of arms,
ammunition, &c., the remnant of the annual trade of
this country, so favoured by nature, and endowed
with such capabilities for commerce, is but £211,834.

There is many a cotton spinner in Manchester
who manufactures much more; there are some
dealers in London whose yearly trade is ten times
that sum; and there is many a merchant in this
country who exports more than the amount of our
whole exports to Africa, arms and ammunition in-
cluded.

The imports from Africa into this country, though
they have, undoubtedly, increased since the year
1820, are still extremely limited; and it is observable that they scarcely embrace any articles produced
from the cultivation of the soil. Their estimated
value, in 1834, was £456,014* (exclusive of gold
dust, about £260,000); they consisted chiefly of
palm-oil, teak timber, gums, ivory, bees'-wax, &c.,

* See Porter's Tables.

all extremely valuable, and in great demand, but obtained at comparatively little labour and cost.

So small an amount of exports from a country so full of mineral and vegetable wealth, either shows the extreme ignorance and indolence of the people, or the total want of security both to person and property which exists in consequence of the Slave Trade. All the authorities which are accessible, clearly show that the latter is the true cause why the commerce between Africa and the civilised world is so trifling; and there is one remarkable fact which corroborates it, namely, that nearly all the legitimate trade with central Africa is effected through the medium of those stations which have been established by the British and French governments on its coasts, and in and around which the trade in slaves has either been greatly checked, or has totally disappeared.

But limited as the commerce of Africa is at present with the civilised world, and infamous as one part of that commerce has been, it is capable of being indefinitely increased, and of having a character impressed on it, alike honourable to all parties engaged in it. The advantages which would accrue to Africa, in the development of her resources, the civilisation of her people, and the destruction of one of the greatest evils which has ever afflicted or disgraced mankind,— not less than the benefits which would be secured to Europe in opening new marts for her produce and new fields for her commercial enterprise—would be incalculable.

What can we do to bring about this consummation ? *It is in our power to encourage her commerce ;—to improve the cultivation of her soil ;—and to raise the morals, and the mind of her inhabitants.* This is all that we can do ; but this done, the Slave Trade cannot continue.

The first question, then, to be considered is, in what way can we give an impulse to the *commerce* of Africa? I apprehend that, for this purpose, little more is necessary than to provide security, and convey a sense of security : without this, there can be no traffic : this alone, with such resources as Africa possesses, will cause legitimate commerce to spring up and thrive of itself; it wants no more than leave to grow. Nothing short of so monstrous an evil as the Slave Trade could have kept it down.

Its natural productions* and commercial re-

---

* PRODUCTIONS.—*Animals.*—Oxen, sheep, goats, pigs, &c., &c., Guinea fowls, common poultry, ducks, &c.

Grain.—Rice, Indian corn, Guinea corn, or millet, wheat, Dourah, &c.

Fruits.—Oranges, lemons, guavas, pines, citrons, limes, papaws, plantains, bananas, dates, &c., &c.

Roots.—Manioc, igname, batalee, yams, arrow-root, ginger, sweet potato, &c., &c.

Timber.—Teak, ebony, lignum vitæ, and forty or fifty other species of wood for all purposes.

Nuts.—Palm-nut, shea-nut, cocoa-nut, cola-nut, ground-nut, castor-nut, netta-nut, &c., &c.

Dyes.—Carmine. yellow various shades, blue, orange various shades, red, crimson, brown, &c.

Dye woods.—Cam-wood, bar-wood, &c., &c.

Gums.—Copal, Senegal, mastic, sudan, &c.

sources are inexhaustible. From the testimony of merchants whose enterprise has, for many years past, led them to embark capital in the African trade ; and from the evidence furnished by the journals of travellers into the interior of the country,* we gather

Drugs.—Aloes, cassia, senna, frankincense, &c.

Minerals.—Gold, iron, copper, emery, sal-ammoniac, nitre, &c.

Sugar-cane, coffee, cotton, indigo, tobacco, India rubber, beeswax, ostrich feathers and skins, ivory, &c.

Fish.—Of an immense variety, and in great abundance.

NOTE.—The above is a very imperfect list, but it may serve to show, at a glance, some of the riches of Africa.   For all the statements relating to Africa, its capabilities and productions, I have specific authorities ; but it seems hardly necessary to quote them.

* I shall here mention some of the names of countries and kingdoms : —

Timbuctoo, the great emporium of trade in central Africa.

The powerful kingdom of *Gago*, 400 Arabic miles from Timbuctoo to the south-east, abounds with corn and cattle.   *Guber*, to the east of Gago, abounds with cattle.   *Cano*, once the famous Ghana, abounds with corn, rice, and cattle.   *Cashna Agadez*, fields abound with rice, millet, and cotton.   *Guangara*, south of this, a region greatly abounding in gold and aromatics.   *Balia*, celebrated for its fine gold, four months' voyage to Timbuctoo. *Bournou*, its capital very large, and inhabitants great traders. The country very rich and fertile, and produces rice, beans, cotton, hemp, indigo in abundance, horses, buffaloes, and horned cattle, sheep, goats, camels, &c.   *Yaoorie* produces abundance of rice. The country between *R. Formosa* and *Adra* affords the finest prospect in the world.   Inland it is healthy, and the climate good. Trees uncommonly large and beautiful, cotton of the finest quality, amazingly plentiful, and indigo and other dye stuffs abundant. The *Jabboos* carry on great trade in grain between *Benin and Lagos.*   *Boossa* is a large emporium for trade.   The place where the people from the sea-coast meet the caravans from Barbary to exchange their merchandise.   From Boossa to Darfur there are numerous powerful, fertile, cultivated, well-wooded, watered, populous, and industrious states.   Benin, Bournou, Dar Saley,

that Nature has scattered her bounties with the most
lavish hand; and that what is required to make them
available to the noblest purposes is a legitimate commerce sustained by the government, and directed by
honourable men.

In the animal kingdom I find that, in addition to the
wild beasts which infest its forests, and occupy its
swamps, and whose skins, &c., are valuable as an
article of commerce, immense herds of cattle, incalculable in number, range its plains. Hides, therefore, to almost any amount, may be obtained; and
well-fed beef, of excellent quality and flavour, can be
obtained at some of our settlements, at from 2*d*. to
3*d*. per lb. There are also in various districts immense flocks of sheep; but as they are covered with

Darfur, Kashua, Houssa, Timbuctoo, Sego, Wassenah, and many
others, are populous kingdoms, abounding in metals, minerals,
fruits, grain, cattle, &c.

Attah, on the Niger, healthy, many natural advantages, will be
a place of great importance, alluvial soil, &c. The places on the
banks of the Niger are rich in sheep, goats, bullocks, &c.

Fundah, population 30,000; beautiful country.

Doma, population large and industrious.

Beeshle and Jacoba, places of great trade.

Rabba, population 40,000.

Toto, population immense.

Alorie (Feletah), vast herds and flocks.

Bumbum, thoroughfare for merchants, from Houssa, Borgoo,
&c., to Gonga, vast quantity of land cultivated.

Gungo (Island), palm-trees in profusion.

Egga, two miles in length; vast number of canoes. Egga to
Bournou, said to be fifteen days' journey.

Tschadda, on its banks immense herds of elephants seen, from
50 to 400 at a time.

a very coarse wool, approaching to hair, and their flesh is not very good on the coast, it may be said, that though numerous, they are not valuable; their skins, however, might form an article for export. Goats of a very fine and large kind are equally numerous, and sell at a lower price than sheep. Their skins are valuable. Pigs can be obtained in any numbers; they are kept at several of the coast stations. Domestic poultry, the Guinea hen, common fowls, ducks, &c., are literally swarming, especially in the interior, and may be had for the most trifling articles in barter both on the coast and inland. Fish of all kinds visit the shores and rivers in immense shoals, and are easily taken in great quantities during the proper season.

The mineral kingdom has not yet been explored, but enough is already known to show that the precious metals abound, particularly gold. The gold-dust obtained from the beds of some rivers, and otherwise produced, is, comparatively, at present, a large branch of the African trade. It is said that gold may be procured in the kingdom of Bambouk, which is watered by the Felema, flowing into the Senegal, and is therefore easily attainable in any quantity. Martin says, (vol. iv., p. 540,) the main depositories where this metal is traced, as it were, to its source, are two mountains, Na Takon and Semayla. In the former, gold is very abundant, and is found united with earth, iron, or emery. In the latter, the gold is imbedded in hard

sandstone.   Numerous streams (he adds) flow from
these districts, almost all of which flow over sands
impregnated with gold.   The natives, unskilled in
mining operations, have penetrated to very little depth
in these mountains.   Park found the mines of the
Konkadoo hills, which he visited, excessively rich, but
very badly worked. (Chapter on gold, vol. i. pp. 454,
465, 524, and vol. ii. pp. 73, 76.)   The gold which
forms the staple commodity of the Gold Coast, is
chiefly brought down from mountains of the interior.
It is said that the whole soil yields gold-dust, and
that small quantities are obtained even in the town of
Cape Coast.*   There are reported to be mines within
twenty or thirty miles of the shore, but the natives are very jealous of allowing Europeans to see
them.†   Dupuis and Bowditch speak of the " solid
lumps of rock gold" which ornament the persons of
the cabooceers in the court of the king of Ashantee,
at Coomassie.‡   Mrs. Lee (late Mrs. Bowditch) says,
that the great men will frequently on state occasions,
so load their wrists with these lumps, that they are
obliged to support them on the head of a boy. The
largest piece she saw at Cape Coast weighed 14 oz.
and was very pure.§   Dupuis, on the authority of
some Mohammedans, says that a great deal of gold
comes from Gaman, and that it is the richest in

* Sierra Leone Report, 1830, p. 87.   † Ib. p. 88.
‡ Dupuis' Ashantee, p. 74 ; Bowditch's Travels, p. 35.
§ " Stories of Strange Lands," p. 66.

Africa.* Gold is said to be discovered in a plain near Houssa; and another writer (Jackson) says— " The produce of Soudan, returned by the akkabuahs, consists principally in gold-dust, twisted gold rings of Wangara, gold rings made at Jinnie (which are invariably of pure gold, and some of them of exquisite workmanship) bars of gold,† &c." He also states that gold-dust is the circulating medium at Timbuctoo.‡

Iron is found in Western Africa. The ore from Sierra Leone is particularly rich, yielding seventy-nine per cent., according to Mr. M'Cormack, and said to be well adapted to making steel.§ The iron brought from Upper Senegal, by Mollien, was found to be of a very good quality. Berthier found it to resemble Catalonian.‖ Iron is found also near Timbuctoo, and is manufactured by the Arabs.¶ The discovery of this important metal in Africa is of the utmost consequence to its future prosperity, and will greatly facilitate the accomplishment of the object contemplated. Early travellers relate that the mountains of Congo are almost all ferruginous, but that the natives have not been encouraged by Europeans to extract their own treasures. Copper is so abundant in Mayomba, that they gather from the surface of the ground enough for their purposes.** Sal ammoniac is found in abund-

* Dupuis, Ap. lvi.　　† Jackson's Timbuctoo, p. 245, 246.
‡ Jackson's Timbuctoo, p. 251.　　§ Sierra Leone Report, 1830.
‖ Mollien's Travels, Appendix.　　¶ Jackson's Timbuctoo, p. 24.
** Degrandpré, T. F., p. 38.

ance in Dagwumba, and is sold cheap in the Ashantee market; nitre, emery, and trona, a species of
alkali, are found on the border of the Desert.* I
might greatly enlarge this list, from the writings of
travellers who have already visited the country, but it
will be long before its mineral wealth will be adequately known.

It is not, however, to the mineral treasures of
Africa that we chiefly look; we regard the productions of the soil as of infinitely more value, especially
those which require industry and skill in their
culture. We look to the forests, and the plains,
and the valleys, and the rich alluvial deltas, which
it would take centuries to exhaust of their fertility
aud products.

Fifty miles to the leeward of the colony, of Sierra
Leone is a vast extent of fertile ground, forming the
delta of the Seeong Boom, Kitiam and Gallinas
rivers. This ground may contain from 1,000 to 1,500
square miles of the richest alluvial soil, capable of
growing all tropical produce. According to Mr.
M‘Cormack, this delta could grow rice enough for
the supply of the whole West Indies.† At present it
produces nothing but the finest description of slaves.‡

* Bowditch, p. 333.

† Sierra Leone Report, No. 66, p. 64.

‡ There is another large delta, formed by the rivers Nunez,
Rio Grande, and Rio Ponga. It is described as very extensive and
fertile. The Isles de Loss command the mouths of these rivers.
The Rio Nunez runs parallel with the Gambia.—*Mr. Laird.*

From Cape St. Paul to Cameroons, and from thence to Cape Lopez, extends the richest country that imagination can conceive. Within this space from forty to fifty rivers of all sizes discharge their waters into the ocean, forming vast flats of alluvial soil, to the extent of 180,000 square miles. From this ground at present the greatest amount of our imports from Western Africa is produced, and to it and the banks of the rivers that flow through it, do I look for the greatest and most certain increase of trade. It is a curious feature in the geography of Africa, that so many of its great navigable rivers converge upon this point (Laird). The extent to which the Slave Trade is carried on in the rivers alluded to is immense, and offers the greatest possible obstruction to the fair trader.

With few inconsiderable exceptions, the whole line of coast in Western Africa, accessible to trading vessels, presents immense tracts of land of the most fertile character, which only require the hand of industry and commercial enterprise to turn them into inexhaustible mines of wealth.

But it is not to the coast alone that the merchant may look for the results of his enterprise. The interior is represented as equally fertile with the coast; and it is the opinion of the most recent travellers, as well as of those who preceded them, that if the labourer were allowed to cultivate the soil in security, the list of productions would embrace all the marketable commodities imported from the East and West Indies.

Between Kacunda and Egga, both large towns on the Niger, the country is described as very fertile, and from Egga to Rabbah, where the river is 3,000 yards wide, the right bank is represented to consist of extensive tracts of cultivated land, with rich and beautiful plains stretching as far as the eye can reach (Laird). The country does not deteriorate as we ascend the river. We have the testimony of Park, corroborated by Denham and Clapperton, in support of this statement, and their remarks embrace both sides of the river. The country surrounding Cape Palmas, the Gambia, the Senegal, the Shary, the Congo, presents to the eye of the traveller unlimited tracts of the most fertile portion of the earth.

The woods of this continent are extremely valuable. Travellers enumerate not less than forty species of timber, which grow in vast abundance, and are easily obtained ; such as mahogany, teak, ebony, lignum vitæ, rosewood, &c.

While Colonel Nicolls was stationed at Fernando Po, he gives this account of its timber, in a letter to Mr. Secretary Hay. I extract the passage as a specimen of the nature of African forests. He says that some of the trees are ten feet in diameter, and 120 feet in height.—" Twenty men have been for a period of eight days cutting down one tree of these dimensions, for the purpose of making a canoe : it

was quite straight, without a branch; the wood
white in colour, close in grain, and very hard. I
have no name for it, but it very much resembles the
lignum vitæ, except in colour. The canoe cut out
of it is five feet within the gunwales, forty feet long,
and carries about twenty tons safely, drawing but
eight inches water. We have also a very fine description of red wood, close-grained, strong, and good
for beams, sheathing, ribs, and deck-planking of the
heaviest vessels of war. We could send home stern-
posts and stems, in one piece, for the largest ships.
This wood seems to have a grain something between
mahogany and oak: when cut thin to mend boats,
it will not split in the sun, and when tapped or cut
down, exudes a tough resinous gum, is very lasting,
and not so heavy as teak or oak, takes a fine polish,
and I think it a very valuable wood. There is
another hard-wood tree of very large dimensions, the
wood strong and good, in colour brown and white-
streaked; it also exudes, when cut, a strong gum,
which I think would be valuable in commerce.
Another, which we call the mast-tree, from the circumstance of its being very tall and straight, is in
colour and grain like a white pine. We have,
besides the above-mentioned trees, many which are
smaller, but very useful, their wood being hard,
tough, and of beautifully variegated colours; some
are streaked brown and white, like a zebra, others of
black, deep red, and brown."

In a despatch, 1832, Colonel Nicolls further

states, that he has Commodore Hayes' authority for saying, that there never was finer wood for the purposes of ship-building.*

Of dye-woods† there are also abundance, yielding

---

* Desp. p. 5; Colonial Records, 1832.

† Many beautiful kinds of wood have been discovered by accident amongst the billets of firewood, brought home in the slave-ships to Liverpool. Mr. Clarkson gives the following anecdote in his " Impolicy of the Slave Trade." After mentioning the tulip-wood and others, found in this manner, he says:—" About the same time in which this log was discovered (A. D. 1787), another wood vessel, belonging to the same port, brought home the specimen of the bark of a tree, that produced a very valuable yellow dye, and far beyond any other ever in use in this country. The virtues of it were discovered in the following manner:—A gentleman, resident upon the coast, ordered some wood to be cut down to erect a hut. While the people were felling it he was standing by : during the operation some juice flew from the bark of it, and stained one of the ruffles of his shirt. He thought that the stain would have washed out, but, on wearing it again, found that the yellow spot was much more bright and beautiful than before, and that it gained in lustre every subsequent time of washing. Pleased with the discovery, which he knew to be of so much importance to the manufacturers of Great Britain, and for which a considerable premium had been offered, he sent home the bark now mentioned as a specimen. He is since unfortunately dead, and little hopes are to be entertained of falling in with this tree again, unless a similar accident should discover it, or a change should take place in our commercial concerns with Africa. I shall now mention another valuable wood, which, like all those that have been pointed out, was discovered by accident in the same year. Another wood vessel, belonging to the same port, was discharging her cargo ; among the barwood a small billet was discovered, the colour of which was so superior to that of the rest, as to lead the observer to suspect, that it was of a very different species, though it is clear that the natives,

carmine, crimson, red, brown, brilliant yellow, and the various shades from yellow to orange, and a fine blue. Of gums there are copal, Senegal mastic, and Sudan, or Turkey gum, to be obtained in large quantities; and there are forests near the Gambia where, hitherto, the gum has never been picked. Of nuts, which are beginning to form a new and important article of trade, there are the palm-nut, the shea-nut, the cola-nut, the ground-nut, the castor-nut, the nitta-nut, and the cocoa-nut. The palm-tree grows most luxuriantly, and incalculable quantities of its produce are allowed to rot on the ground for want of gathering; yet it is now the most important branch of our commerce with Africa, and may be increased to any extent. The oil expressed from its nut is used in the manufacture of soap and candles, and in lubricating machinery. The shea, or butter-nut,* is scarcely less

by cutting it of the same size and dimensions, and by bringing it on board at the same time, had, on account of its red colour, mistaken it for the other. One half of the billet was cut away in experiments. It was found to produce a colour that emulated the carmine, and was deemed to be so valuable in the dyeing trade, that an offer was immediately made of sixty guineas per ton for any quantity that could be procured. The other half has been since sent back to the coast, as a guide to collect more of the same sort, though it is a matter of doubt whether, under the circumstances that have been related, the same tree can be ascertained again."—p. 9.

* The butter is prepared by boiling, and besides the advantage of keeping a whole year without salt, it is " whiter, firmer, and, to my palate," says Park (vol. i. p. 302), " of a richer

valuable than the palm-nut. Some travellers inform their readers that it is an excellent substitute for butter and can be appropriated to the same uses with the palm-oil. It is a remarkable fact, in the natural history of these trees, that immediately where the one ceases to yield its fruit, the other flourishes abundantly. The ground-nut* is becoming also a valuable article of commerce; and this with the other nuts mentioned, yield a rich supply of oil and oil-cake for the use of cattle. The value of the castor-nut, as an article of medicine, needs not be particularly adverted to. The roots which grow in Africa require generally but little attention in their cultivation; among others, there are the following:—The manioc, yams, sweet potatoes, arrow-

flavour than the best butter I ever tasted made of cow's milk." The shea-tree, which produces it, is said to extend over a large part of the continent, from Jaloof to Gaboon. " It has been analysed by the French chemist, M. Chevreuil, and found well adapted for the manufacture of soap. Being inodorous and highly capable of taking a perfume, it would be valuable for the finer sorts."— Mrs. Lee, *Stories of Strange Lands*, p. 26.

* The *ground-nut* yields a pure golden-coloured oil, of a pleasant taste, and has been sold here at 56*l.* per ton. From 750 to 1000 tons are produced on the Gambia; but these nuts appear plentiful along the whole coast, are often mentioned by Park, and were noticed by Denham, as very abundant near the lake Tchad. It grows in a soil too light and sandy for corn—its stalks afford fodder for cattle—it sells at six shillings per gallon, and is as good as sperm-oil. The *castor-nut* also grows wild in great abundance on the banks of the Gambia, and elsewhere.

root, and ginger :* the two latter are exportable, and the former yield a large amount of healthful and nutritious food. Yams can be so improved by cultivation that, at Fernando Po, Captain Bullen says, many weigh from fifteen to twenty-five pounds, and in taste almost equal a potato. On one occasion he bought upwards of four tons for seventy-six iron hoops; and says, " The nourishment derived from them to my people was beyond belief."† The fruits are oranges, lemons, citrons, limes, pines, guavas, tamarinds, paw-paws, plantains and bananas. The paw-paw and plantain trees (says Ashmun) are a good example of the power of an uniformly-heated climate to accelerate vegetation. You may see in the gardens many of the former, not more than fifteen months from the seed, already fifteen inches round the stem, and fifteen feet high, with several pecks of ripening fruit. Clear your lands, plant your crops, keep the weeds down, and the most favourable climate in the world, alone, under the direction of a bountiful Providence, will do more for you than all your toil and care could accomplish in America."‡ Tamarinds are

---

* The ginger of Africa is particularly fine, and high flavoured; it yields about sixty for one; and the people only want instruction in the method of preparing it for European markets.—*Denham, Desp.*, 21st *May*, 1827; *Sierra Leone Report*, 1830, *No.* 57, p. 30.

† Captain Bullen's Desp., November, 1826

‡ Ashmun's Life, Ap. p. 66.

exportable. Of grain, there is rice, Indian corn, Guinea corn, or millet, &c. The quantities of these can be raised to any extent, and be limited only by demand.* The Rev. W. Fox, the Missionary, says, in his MS. Journal, August 22, 1836—" This afternoon I visited Laming, a small Mandingo town (above Macarthy's Island). I could scarcely get into the town for the quantity of Indian corn with which it is surrounded; upon a very moderate calculation, and for a very small portion of labour, which generally devolves upon the poor women, they reap upwards of two hundred fold." I am informed that Madeira wholly depends on the maize raised in Africa, and that the rice produced there, when properly dried and prepared, is equal to that grown in South Carolina. Of drugs, there are aloes† and cassia, senna, frankincense, cardamums, and grains of paradise, or Malagetta pepper. Amongst the miscellaneous products, which

* " Nothing can be more delightful than a stroll along the borders of the beautiful fields, winding occasionally along almost impervious clusters of young palms, whose spreading branches exclude every ray of the scorching sun, then opening suddenly on an immense rice-field of the most delicate pea-green, skirted by the beautiful broad-leaved plantain and banana, literally groaning under the immense masses of their golden fruit." Dr. J. Hall, Governor of Liberia. *Missionary Register*, 1836, p. 360.

† A new use of the aloe plant has been discovered in the beautiful tissue and cordage manufactured from its fibres, by M. Pavy, of Paris. The fibres of the palm and banana-trees are also wrought by him into glossy stuffs.

are in great demand in this country, may be enume-
rated ivory, bees'-wax, caoutchouc, or Indian-rubber.
The former of these articles will, of course, suffer a
gradual diminution as the forests are cut down, the
swamps, drained, and the plains cultivated; but of
the latter scarcely any diminution need be appre-
hended. The bees'-wax of Africa is in great
repute, and can be had in any quantity; and the
great price freely given for Indian-rubber might be
a sufficient inducement to lead the African to pay
more attention to its collection. Of this Mr. Rankin says,* describing what he saw in an excursion
amongst the Timmanese,—" A large lump of Indian-rubber (caoutchouc) lay on the table, also the
produce of Tombo. This article, at present acquiring a high value amongst our importations, is
not there made an article of commerce, Like almost every other produce of the neighbourhood of
Sierra Leone, it is scarcely known to exist, or is
entirely neglected. It grows plentifully, and may
be easily obtained by making incisions into the tree,
from which it flows like cream, into calabashes tied
underneath; it hardens within a few hours."

Mr. Elliot Cresson, examined before the American
Committee on the Foreign Slave Trade, February,
1839, stated, in answer to the question,—" What
will be the commercial and political advantages to
the United States, from an intercourse with the
colony of Liberia?" " Among the valuable articles

* Rankin's Sierra Leone, vol. ii. p. 218.

of export, wax and spices are obtained in large quantities in our colony. The India-rubber tree grows wild in the neighbouring woods, and ostrich feathers have been exported largely. Hides could be obtained in any quantities ; so could rosewood, lancewood, and palmwood, and live oak of the best quality. One merchant in Philadelphia last year imported from the colony a quantity of pea or ground nuts, from which he realised the profit of 12,000 dollars. Cotton, of a very good staple, is found there, and cultivated with great advantage, as there is no frost there. And the articles desired in return are those produced by American manufactures and agriculture."—*Colonization Herald*, March, 1839, p. 124.

Ashmun, who seems to have had a clear view of the interest of the Liberian settlers, writes to them thus :—" Suffer me to put down two or three remarks, of the truth and importance of which you cannot be too sensible. The first is, that the cultivation of your rich lands is the only way you will ever find out to independence, comfort, and wealth." " You may, if you please, if God gives you health, become as independent, comfortable, and happy as you ought to be in this world." " The flat lands around you, and particularly your farms, have as good a soil as can be met with in any country. They will produce two crops of corn, sweet potatoes, and several other vegetables, in a year. They will yield a larger crop than the best soils in America. And they will produce a number of very valuable articles, for which in the

United States, millions of money are every year paid away to foreigners. One acre of rich land, well tilled, will produce you three hundred dollars' worth of indigo. Half an acre may be made to grow half a ton of arrow-root. Four acres laid out in coffee-plants, will, after the third year, produce you a clear income of two or three hundred dollars. Half an acre of cotton-trees will clothe your whole family; and, except a little hoeing, your wife and children can perform the whole labour of cropping and manufacturing it. One acre of canes will make you independent of all the world for the sugar you use in your family. One acre set with fruit-trees, and well attended, will furnish you the year round with more plantains, bananas, oranges, limes, guavas, papaws, and pine-apples, than you will ever gather. Nine months of the year, you may grow fresh vegetables every month, and some of you who have lowland plantations, may do so throughout the year." *

I must also quote the authority of Denis de Montfort, a Frenchman of science, who in a paper on the gold of the Coast of Guinea, inserted in the " Philosophical Magazine," thus writes:—" There exists no country in the world so susceptible of general cultivation as Africa : we know that certain districts are fertile in corn ; and grain of every kind grows there, intermixed with sugar-canes lately introduced, and which protect the grain from hail. The plants of India, Europe, America, and Australia

* Ashmun's Life, Ap., p. 64.

will flourish there in perpetual spring, and the animals of all climates can be easily naturalised. The negroes, whose respect for the whites is extreme, notwithstanding what they have suffered from them, will cheerfully give up their fields to be cultivated by them. Servants, and even slaves, will not be wanting, and this will be a true method of preventing these nations from massacring their prisoners of war, as the king of Dahomey does at the present moment. May our feeble voices on this subject reach the ear of royalty! *

It is almost impossible to turn to any book of African travels, without meeting with some incidental observations upon the fertility of the soil. I should have supposed that nothing of this kind would have occurred in the narrative of Captain Paddock; yet he says:—" On the south was seen a very extensive country, abounding with little enclosed cities, large fields of grain, and productive gardens. In short, though the climate here is dry as well as hot, such is the great fertility of the soil, that it is capable of producing abundantly all the necessaries and most of the luxuries of life. What might it be under the cultivation of a civilised, industrious, and skilful people!†

" We made choice of a wheat-field, which lay but a few hundred yards from us; and we had entered it but a few paces when we found ourselves completely hidden, even while standing erect. Although my mate was five feet eleven inches in height, and myself

---

* Annual Register, 1815, p. 542.   † P. 289.

five feet ten, the heads of the wheat were above our own. This was the finest piece of wheat I ever saw; it was all well headed; and had we not gone among it, and took its measure, we should have known it was very tall, though we never could have told how tall." *

It is observed by Brown, in his botanical appendix to " Tuckey's Voyage " (pp. 342-3), that from the river Senegal, in about 16° north latitude, to the Congo, in upwards of 6° south latitude, there is a remarkable uniformity in the vegetation of Western Africa—a fact which gives us promise of extending to any amount, our commerce in such vegetable productions as have already obtained a sale in Europe or America. Thus a tree which characterises nearly the whole range of coast, is the Elais Guineensis, or oil-palm, one of the most valuable to commerce. This grows in the greatest abundance in the delta of the Niger. There " the palm-nut now rots on the ground unheeded and neglected," over an extent of surface equal to the whole of Ireland. (Laird, vol. ii. p. 362.)

The whole extent, too, of the Timmanee, and a great part of Koranko, through which Captain Laing passed in 1822, was absolutely bristled with palm-trees, which, at the time he went up the country (April and May), were bearing luxurious crops of nuts. " There is no known instance, or any apparent danger, of a failure on the part of all-bountiful nature in supplying the fruit : on the contrary, it

* P. 181.

is the opinion of Captain Laing, that were the population double, and had they all the industry we could wish, they would not be able to reap the abundant harvest annually presented to them."*

The soil of Africa produces indigenously nearly all the useful plants which are common to other tropical countries, and some of them in greater perfection than they are to be found elsewhere.

There are some articles that require more notice:

Hemp grows wild on the Gambia, and only requires a better mode of preparation to make it a valuable article of import. The same may be said of tobacco. Indigo grows so freely in Africa, that, in some places, it is difficult to eradicate it. " Immense quantities of indigo, and other noxious weeds," spring up in the streets of Freetown.†

It is known to grow wild as far inland as the Tchad, and even with the rude preparation bestowed by the natives, gives a beautiful dye to their cloths.‡

Coffee is another indigenous shrub, which well repays cultivation. When Kizell, a Nova Scotian, first observed it near the Sherbro, he pulled up two or three plants, and showed them to the people, who said that they thought it was good for nothing, but to fence their plantations. It was all over the country, and in some places nothing else was to be

* Sierra Leone Gaz., Dec. 14, 1822.

† Despatch, Mr. Smart to Sir G. Murray, 1828; Sierra Leone Report, No. 57, p. 30.

‡ Denham's Travels, p. 246.

seen.* Even in a wild state it seems to repay the trouble of gathering, for the Commissioners at Sierra Leone, in their Annual Report, of date 1st January, 1838, inform us " that the Foulahs have been induced, by the fair traders of the river Nunez to bring down for sale to them a quantity of coffee, of a very superior quality, the produce of the forests of their own country." An extract of a letter, which they enclose, observes that " one great advantage of peaceful commerce with the natives is, that valuable productions of their country are brought to light by our research, sometimes to their astonishment." Thus, till within the last two years, this abundant growth of coffee was " left to be the food of monkeys," but is now a source of profit to the natives and to our own merchants. A small quantity has been cultivated, both at Sierra Leone and the Gold Coast; and Ashmun (Life, Ap., p. 78) states that, in Liberia, no crop is surer; that African coffee frequently produces four pounds to the tree, and that the berries attain a size unknown elsewhere. I am happy to learn that above 10,000 lbs. of African coffee were imported into this country in 1837, that its quality was excellent, and that it fetched a good price.†

---

* Afr. Inst 6 Report, Ap.

† Mr. M'Queen says, that the old Arabian traveller Batouta, who had visited China, states, that in the interior parts of Africa, along the Niger, which he visited, the tea-plant grew abundantly.— M'Queen's *Africa*, p. 218. Dr. M'Leod, describing the kingdom of Benin, says—" In the opinion of one of the latest governors

Sugar-canes grow spontaneously in several parts of Africa; and when cultivated, as they are in various places, for the sake of the juice, they become very large. The expense of the necessary machinery alone seems to have hitherto prevented the manufacture of sugar;*

I now come to the article which demands the largest share of our attention, viz. cotton; because it requires little capital, yields a steady return, is in vast demand in Europe, and grows naturally in the soil of Africa.

As this last is a point of vital importance, I think it necessary to furnish a portion of the evidence I have collected as to the luxuriant and spontaneous growth of cotton in Africa:—

Sir Fulk Grevell making, by order of Queen Elizabeth, a report to Sir Francis Walsingham on a memorial of certain merchant adventures:—" Sir, You demaunde of me the names of such kings as are absolute in the East, and either have warr or traffique wth the kinge of Spaigne."　　*　*　*　*
" Then followeth kingdoms of Gaulata, *Tombuto,* and Melly; whereof the firste is poore, and hath smal traffique; *the seconde populous, and rich in*

---

we have had, on the establishment in this country (Mr. James), and one whose general knowledge of Africa is admitted to be considerable, the tea-tree flourishes spontaneously here."— M'Leod's *Voyage to Africa,* p. 18.

　* A company has been established at Mourovia, with a small capital, for the experiment.—Col. Herald, November, 1837.

corne and beasts, but wanteth salte, wch the *Por-tugal* supplieth; the last hath store of corne, flesh, and *cotten woll,* wch are *carried into Spaigne* in great abundance." Quoted by Mr. Bruce, from a M.S. in the State Paper Office—Annals of the East India Company, vol. i., p. 121.

Beaver says, " Of the vegetables that are wild, the sugar-cane, cotton-shrub, and indigo-plant, seem the most valuable : no country in the world is more amply enriched than this is with the chief productions of the animal and vegetable kingdoms."

Mr. Dalrymple, who was at Goree in 1779, states, " that there are three different kinds of cotton; that samples sent home were considered by English mer-chants superior to that from the West Indies. It grows spontaneously almost everywhere, though it is sometimes cultivated."[*]

Cotton, says Col. Denham, grows wild about Sierra Leone, of three kinds, white, brown, and pink; the first is excellent.[†] He also "found it wild on the Tschadda."[‡]

Clapperton, saw some " beautiful specimens" of the African looms in the interior.[§]

Park[||] observes, almost every slave can weave.

[*] Evid. Slave Trade Com., 1790, p. 297.
[†] Col. Denham, Rep. Sierra Leone, Sess. 1830, No. 57, p. 16.
[‡] Denham's Travels, p. 317.
[§] Clapperton, p. 5.
[||] Park, vol. i. p 429.

Ashmun* says, it is believed that none of the varieties of the American cotton-shrub answers, in all respects, to the indigenous African tree. The cotton of this country is on all hands allowed to be of a good quality, and the mode of growing, curing, and manufacturing the article pursued in America may be adopted here, making due allowance for the much greater size and duration of the African tree.

Lander says, " From Badagry to Saccatoo, the cotton-plant, indigo, &c., are cultivated to a great extent."

Laird says, "The increase of trade from the interior would, I think, consist chiefly of palm-oil, raw cotton, shea-butter, rice, and bees'-wax. These articles would, I think, be indefinitely increased."

The Rev. John Pinney,† an American missionary, says, " The crops of coffee, pepper, and cotton exceed all that could be boasted of in the United States."

And the Rev. J. Seys‡ speaks of the " excellent cotton" of the St. Paul's River.

I might, if it were necessary, multiply these proofs almost indefinitely, by references to M'Queen, Burckhardt, De Caillë, Dupuis, Robertson, &c.

It has been my endeavour, throughout the whole of this work, to take nothing for granted, and to

* Ashmun's Life, App., p. 76.
† Coloniz. Soc. Rep., quoted in Miss. Reg. for 1836, p. 22.
‡ Ibid.

prove, as I proceeded, all that I stated. It cannot be necessary, however, to stop for the purpose of establishing the vast importance to Great Britain of an additional market for the purchase of raw cotton. In our cotton-trade, there are about twenty millions of fixed, and twenty millions of floating capital invested. The total yearly produce of the manufacture amounts to forty millions. One million five hundred thousand persons earn their bread by it.

Africa is capable of yielding this necessary article : it is as near to us as North America ; nearer than the Brazils ; two-thirds nearer to us than India. The vast tropical districts along the southern side of the Great Desert, the fine plains, and gently-rising country from the northern bank of the Rio de Formosa, and from the Niger to the base of the Kong mountains, are adapted to the culture and production of the finest cotton. This portion of Africa alone, so rich in soil, so easy of access, offers an independent and abundant supply of that article, the want of which impedes and oppresses our manufacturing prosperity. But if Africa, when delivered from that evil which withers her produce, and paralyzes her industry, can be made to supply us with the commodity which we so much need, she, in her turn, will be the customer of Europe to the same vast extent, for the manufactured goods which Europe produces. If it be true that intercourse with Africa, of an honest description, would be twice blessed,—a blessing to the nation who con-

fers, and to the continent which receives, cultivation
and commerce,—nothing can exceed the folly (except the wickedness) of a system, which annually
sweeps off nearly half a million of the inhabitants of
Africa, and consigns, by its inhuman butcheries, one
of the fairest portions of the earth to the sterility of a
wilderness.

But it may be said, that though the land might be
made to produce cotton, centuries must elapse before
it can be made to yield any quantity of that article.
I do not pretend to say that this will be suddenly
accomplished; but an anecdote which I heard stated
to the Marquis of Normanby, by a gentleman whose
mercantile knowledge would not be disputed by
any one, may serve to forbid despair. He stated
that the person who first imported from America a
bale of cotton into this country was still alive, that the
person to whom it was consigned in Liverpool was
still alive, and that the custom-house officer at that
place refused to admit it at the lower rate of duty,
because, to his knowledge, no cotton could be grown
in America; yet that country which could grow no
cotton, now, besides supplying her own demand, and
that of all other countries, sends annually to Great Britain a quantity valued at about £15,000,000 sterling.

I propose, then, that an effort shall be made to cultivate districts of Africa, selected for that purpose,
in order that her inhabitants may be convinced of the

capabilities of their soil, and witness what wonders
may be accomplished by their own labour when set in
motion by our capital, and guided by our skill.

There is no doubt that mercantile settlements
would effect a considerable measure of good; but
the good is distant, and will be effected by slow degrees, while the condition of Africa is such, that the
delay of a single year carries with it a world of
misery, and the certain destruction of a multitude of
lives.

I confess that I think it would be well, on many
grounds, if we could, to confine ourselves to the establishment of factories. I fear, however, that this
limitation would retard, if not defeat, our objects.

We should touch Africa at a few prominent points,
—at each of these, a mart might be established, and
something might be done towards the education of
the children of those who entered our service. But
the evil is gigantic, and it requires gigantic efforts to
arrest it. I believe,—and every word that I have read
or heard on the subject confirms me in the impression,—that Africa has, within herself, resources,
which, duly developed, would compensate for the
gains of the Slave Trade, if these were twenty times
as great as they are. But it must never be forgotten
that these resources are nothing, unless they are fairly
and fully called into action.

Factories on the coast may lead the natives to
gather the spontaneous productions of nature. They
may supply us with wood, with palm-oil, with skins,

and with ivory; but beyond the money or the goods paid for these, and beyond occasional and very lax employment to the natives, Africa would gain little. No habits of settled industry will be inspired; no examples will be placed before those, the avenue to whose understanding is through the eyes; and who however slow they may be to reason, are quick to perceive, and intelligent to imitate.

I have already said, that two things must be achieved, or we shall fail : the one is, to call forth and elevate the native mind ; the other is, to provide a larger source of revenue than that derived from the trade in man.

By agriculture—both will be accomplished. The ransom for Africa will be found in her fertile soil ; and the moral worth of her people will advance as they become better instructed, more secure, more industrious, and more wealthy. And then will be felt the influence of cultivated intellect on rude reason ; the children will be taught by our schools; our very machinery, doing easily what is impossible to their unaided strength, will eloquently speak to others, and beget that allegiance of mind, which is uniformly yielded by the untutored, to beings of superior capacity. The ministers of the gospel, the best of civilizers, will, as gently as irresistibly, work out a change in the current of opinion, and effect the cheerful renunciation of bloody and licentious customs.

Such essential reforms as these cannot be expected from the mere establishment of factories on the coast.

Something, no doubt, will be gained by these, but not enough, to execute the task (of all tasks the most difficult) of giving an impulse to the slumbering energies of the people, and making productive the latent capabilities of the soil. In one word, Africa wants more than commerces—he wants cultivation.

If cultivation be required, it becomes at once desirable that we should afford to the natives the benefit of our experience and skill—our example and capital. Why should the African be left to work his way upwards, from his rude and unprofitable tillage, to that higher order of cultivation, which we have reached by the labours of successive generations? Our discoveries in tropical agriculture must work a great physical change. It is probable, that we might reclaim a waste district in half the time, and at half the expense, that it would cost the inhabitants.

But I look also, as I have already hinted, to the *moral* effect which will hence be produced. Those of old, who carried the spade and the plough into barbarous countries were ranked with the deities.

By our seeds, and our implements, and our skill in abridging labour and subduing difficulty, we shall place before the natives, in a form which they cannot mistake, the vast benefits they are likely to derive from intercourse with us; and they will speedily perceive, that it is their interest to protect those strangers who possess secrets, which can make their land produce so unexpected and rich a harvest.

It is quite clear that the present commercial

intercourse between this country and Africa is
extremely limited ; that the chief obstacle to its
extension is the prevalence of the Slave Trade,* and

* The imports of palm-oil have diminished during four late
years, as may be seen by the following returns, viz. : —

				Cwts.
1834	.	.	.	269,907
1835	.	.	.	234,882
1836	.	.	.	236,195
1837	.		.	201,906

This diminution has arisen, not in consequence of a decrease in
the demand for the article, but on account of the extension of the
Slave Trade on the coast, and the increased difficulty of procuring
a supply.

"The industry of the natives, in a great degree, is stifled by the
Slave Trade; and, though a good deal of oil is prepared and sold,
the English traders, loading at the mouth of the river, are often
interrupted, and obliged to wait, to the loss of profit and the ruin
of the crew's health, while a smuggling slaver takes all hands on
the coast to complete her cargo."—*Laird.*

"When there is a demand for slaves the natives abandon every
other employment ; and the consequence is, that the British vessels
trading on the coast are lying idle for want of trade.

"In consequence of the great demand for slaves, the natives
here and in the interior abandon cultivation, the trees go to destruction, and no young trees are planted.

"At one place in Africa where a very considerable quantity of
palm-oil has been annually supplied to the ships of our merchants,
the Spanish and Portuguese have latterly so much increased the
Slave Trade, that the cultivation of the palm-trees, which was
giving occupation to thousands, has not only become neglected,
but the native chiefs have been incited to blind revenge against
British influence, and have set fire to and destroyed 30,000 palm
trees."—*Recent Letters from Africa.*

that it might be indefinitely increased under the fostering and protective care of the British government. The grounds on which this supposition rests are the number and situation of its navigable rivers; its rich alluvial deltas, and extensive and fertile plains; its immense forests; its wide range of natural productions; its swarming, active, and enterprising population; its contiguity to Europe, and the demand of its people for the manufactures of this country.

In speculating on African commerce, it should be borne in mind that we have to deal with nations who are not only ignorant and uncivilised, but corrupted and deteriorated by the Slave Trade, and by intercourse with the worst class of Europeans. There will, therefore, be difficulties and obstructions to overcome before a clear field for honest commerce can be obtained. In the present state of the people we can hardly look to obtain from them articles which depend on an extensive cultivation of the soil, so as to compete with the productions of civilised nations. It is probable that in commencing an extensive intercourse with Africa, there will be at first a considerable outlay of money without an immediate return; but from whatever source this may be obtained, it should be considered as a gift to Africa. It will ultimately be repaid a thousand-fold.

The articles desired by the Africans in return for the produce of their country are too many to enumerate. Lists of them are given by almost every traveller. It may, therefore, suffice to observe, that

many of them are the produce or manufactures of
our island, or of our colonies ; and it is an important
consideration, that we may obtain the treasures of this
unexplored continent, by direct barter of our own
commodities, and that, while we cheapen luxuries
at home, we also increase the means of obtaining
them, by giving increased employment to our productive classes.

The extension of a legitimate commerce, and with it
the blessings of civilisation and Christianity, is worthy
the most strenuous exertions of the philanthropist,
whilst to the mercantile and general interests of the
civilised world it is of the highest importance. Africa
presents an almost boundless tract of country, teeming with inhabitants who admire, and are desirous of
possessing our manufactures. There is no limit to
the demand, except their want of articles to give us
in return. They must be brought to avail themselves
of their own resources.

Attempts, as we have seen, have already been
made to form cotton plantations, and the article produced is found to be of a very useful and valuable
description. Perseverance in these efforts is alone
required to accomplish the object in view, and, when
once accomplished, the importance to this country
will be incalculable. The trade in palm-oil is capable
of immense extension, and the article is every year
becoming more important and in more extensive
use. In exchange for these, and many other valuable
articles, British manufactures would be taken, and

British ships find a profitable employment in the conveyance of them.

It so happens that a considerable proportion of the goods which best suit the taste of the natives of Africa, consists of fabrics to which power-looms cannot be applied with any advantage. Any extension, then, of the trade to Africa, will have this most important additional advantage, that it will cause a corresponding increase in the demand for the labour of a class of individuals who have lately been truly represented as suffering greater privations than any other set of workmen connected with the cotton trade.

But the first object of our intercourse with Africa should be, not so much to obtain a remunerating trade, as to repair in some measure the evil that the civilised world has inflicted on her, by conveying Christianity, instruction, and the useful arts to her children. The two objects will eventually, if carried on in a right manner, be found perfectly compatible; for it is reasonable to seek in legitimate commerce a direct antidote to the nefarious traffic which has so long desolated and degraded her. We have shown the vast variety and importance of the productions which Africa is capable of yielding: we have already proved that, notwithstanding the bounty of nature, the commerce of Africa is most insignificant. Truly may we say with Burke, " To deal and traffic—not in the labour of men, but in men themselves—is to devour the root, instead of enjoying the fruit of human diligence."

CHAPTER III.

FACILITIES FOR COMMERCIAL INTERCOURSE.

I HAVE thus stated what I conceive to be the gist of
the whole question, viz., that the deliverance of Africa
must spring, under the blessing of God, from herself
and I have also shown, I trust to the satisfaction of
every reader, that she possesses abundant capabilities
for the purpose. The next question that arises, is,
how are these capabilities to be made available? how
are we to obtain access to them? Great, no doubt, are
the difficulties; yet, such are the discoveries of the last
ten years, that we may now lay aside the impressions
of an impenetrable continent, and of interminable
wastes of sand, which have accompanied us from our
childhood. We now know that a mighty river,
which discharges itself into the Bight of Benin, by
upwards of twenty mouths, is navigable, with little
interruption, from thence nearly to its source, a
distance of more than 2,600 miles. We also learn
from the travellers who have navigated the Niger,
that there are many tributary streams, some of which,
especially the Tschadda, or Shaderbah, are equally
navigable, and afford every facility for intercourse
with the numerous nations and tribes who inhabit
the countries in their vicinity.

Mungo Park, in his last journey (1805), embarked on the Niger at Bammakoo, about 500 miles from its source. In his narrative he says, " Having gained the summit of the ridge which separates the Niger from the remote branches of the Senegal, I went on a little before, and coming to the brow of the hill, *I once more saw the Niger* rolling its immense stream along the plain." And he tells us, it is larger " even here, than either the Senegal or the Gambia, and full an English mile over." When preparing for his subsequent embarkation on the Niger, he says, " the best wood for boat-building is near Kaukary, on a large navigable branch of the Niger." Park descended the river to Boussa, where most unhappily he was killed.

In 1830, Lander, who had accompanied the enterprising Clapperton in his last journey to Houssa, was sent out by the British Government to explore the Niger. He succeeded in reaching Boussa by a land route: there he embarked on the river, and after a voyage of about 560 miles, reached the Bight of Benin, and thus solved the interesting problem which had so long exercised the talents and ingenuity of modern geographers.

Messrs. Laird and Oldfield, by the aid of steam-vessels, went up the Niger from the Bight of Benin, in 1832; and their journals contain much valuable information as to that river, and its tributary, the Tschadda. The latter, at the point of confluence, is represented to be one mile and a half broad; and the country on the banks of both rivers is described to be most fertile, very populous, and, wherever there is any security from the ravages of the Slave Trade, highly cultivated.

Mr. Oldfield ascended the Niger to the town of Rabbah, and he explored the Tschadda, for about 100 miles from its confluence with the Niger at Addacuddah.

They also describe several towns, Eboe, Iccory, Iddah, Egga, Rabbah, and Fundah, proving how great are the facilities for trade and commerce with the interior afforded by the river.

It is to be regretted that so little of the Tschadda has been explored. Mr. Oldfield was informed, that its course lay through the heart of Africa, and that there were many large towns on its banks; and Laird in mentioning this river, says, " By it, a communication would be opened with all the nations inhabiting the unknown countries between the Niger and the Nile."

Here, then, is one of the most magnificent rivers in the world, introducing us into the heart of Africa : at a central point, it opens a way by its eastern branch, to the kingdoms of Bornou, Kanem, and Begharmi; by its western, to Timbuctoo,—each of them bringing us into communication with multitudes of tribes, and unfolding to us the productions of a most extensive and fertile territory.

The problem is, how shall that stream be closed to the passage of slaves to the coast; while it is at the same time opened as a secure and accessible highway for legitimate commerce. The solution seems almost self-evident : we must obtain the positions which command the Niger ; and without doubt, the most important of these, is Fernando Po.

FERNANDO PO.

I have already adverted to the importance of this island, as being decidedly the best locality on the coast for the reception of liberated negroes; and for aiding us in a great effort for the civilization of Africa. It is situated about 20 miles from the mainland, in the Bight of Biafra, and commands the mouths of those great streams which penetrate so deeply into central Africa, along the coast from the Rio Volta to the Gaboon. These rivers are about forty in number, and Fernando Po is at the distance of from 40 to 200 miles. The island is exceedingly fertile; the soil is composed of a fine deep black and brick mould: it abounds in many species of large and fine timber, fit for ornamental or useful purposes; and it is capable of producing, in the highest perfection, not only every article of tropical produce, but also many kinds of European fruits and vegetables: it is 24 miles in length, and 16 miles in breadth. It has three ranges of hills, running parallel to the north-east side; the centre rising into a conical volcanic mountain, to the height of 10,000 feet above the level of the sea.

Mr. Laird thus describes its aspect:—" On my

F

return to Fernando Po I recovered rapidly, and was able to walk and ride about in a fortnight after my arrival. The splendid scenery that distinguishes this beautiful island is well known from former descriptions, and to persons coming from the low marshy shore of the main land has indescribable charms.

"The view from the galleries of the government-house on a clear moonlight night I never saw equalled, nor can I conceive it surpassed. To the north-east, the lofty peak of the Camaroons, rising to the immense height of 14,000 feet, throws its shadow halfway across the narrow strait that separates the island from the main land; while the numerous little promontories, and beautiful coves, that grace the shores of Goderich Bay, throw light and shadow so exquisitely upon the water, that one almost can imagine it a fairy land. On the west, the spectator looks down almost perpendicularly on the vessels in Clarence Cove, which is a natural basin, surrounded by cliffs of the most romantic shape, and a group of little islands, which nature seems to have thrown in, to give a finish to the scene.

"Looking inland, towards the island, the peak is seen, covered with wood to the summit, with its sides furrowed with deep ravines, and here and there a patch of cleared land, showing like a white spot in the moonlight."

We are also informed, that, from the elevation of 3,500 feet above the level of the sea, there is always found the climate of an European summer.

The shores are bold, and, with hardly an exception, free from those swamps on the coasts of the main land, around the mouths of the rivers, which generate the fatal malaria which proves so destructive to the health and life of Europeans. From all this Fernando Po is entirely free; while the land remains uncleared and uncultivated, diseases, the attendants of every tropical climate, will, to a considerable extent prevail, but never equal to what is witnessed on the alluvial, flooded, and swampy shores of the adjacent continent. When, however, the land shall be cleared and cultivated, the climate, we may reasonably expect, will become healthy and safe for Europeans: the same as the climate is found to be in the elevated parts of Jamaica, and in those West Indian islands which are cleared, cultivated, and drained, such as Barbadoes and St. Christopher's, to the latter of which Fernando Po bears in many points a very strong resemblance. The putrid malaria, generated on the alluvial plains and swamps, on the shores of the sea, and in the neighbourhood of large rivers in the torrid zone, never rises to any great height, probably not 400 feet above the level of the sea at any place; and, consequently, it is very obvious that Fernando Po would, when cleared of the wood, afford a healthy, as well as convenient location for any British force, or settlement, which it may be considered necessary or advisable to place upon it. The island, moreover, is free from hurricanes: there are several bays which afford most convenient access: two of these, North West Bay

F 2

and Maidstone Bay, were carefully surveyed by
Commodore Bullen in 1826.   He describes the latter
bay, as perfectly easy of access, and at once healthy
and very airy, the westerly wind blowing directly
across it at all times of day and night.   He also says
that there is good anchorage in all parts of the bay;
that it abounds with fish and turtle; and that many
streams of excellent water run into it.   There are
in this bay two very fine coves, where ships might lie
and refit, as smooth as in a mill-pond, combined with
the benefit of a beautiful and refreshing breeze.
Commodore Bullen further says, that if a look-out be
kept from the shore of this bay, scarcely a vessel
could leave the Bonny, Calabars, Bimbia, and Camaroons rivers, without being observed time enough to
give a signal to any vessel lying in the bay to intercept
her; and he cites as an instance, the capture of a
slaver, "Le Daniel," by his own vessel.   This capture was effected within four hours after first seeing
her, although his vessel was then lying at anchor in
the bay.   Commodore, now Sir Charles Bullen,
strongly recommended that a settlement should be
formed for liberated Africans in Maidstone Bay; but
it appears that Clarence Cove was preferred.   Of the
latter place we are told, that it affords the finest shelter
and anchorage for shipping; 500 sail may there ride
in perfect safety and lie quite close to the shore.   It
also abounds with excellent spring water, as in fact
the island generally does; the fine streams rushing
from the mountains to the sea, in beautiful waterfalls

and cascades, down its bold coasts. " You have not,"
said a gentleman, who had resided there nine years,
and whose testimony may be relied upon, " an island,
either in the North or South Atlantic, equal to Fernando Po for shipping: a vessel may anchor there
all the year round in perfect safety."

Colonel Nichols computes the natives to amount to
about 5,000; and he states that, if the island were
cleared and cultivated, it could easily maintain a very
large population. He found the natives friendly,
inoffensive, and willing to work : he employed them
in clearing the ground for the British settlement at
Clarence Cove.

The Colonel speaks in high terms of the products
and capabilities of the island. The yams were the
finest he ever saw, and he introduced the cultivation
of Indian corn with complete success; and Captain
Beatty thinks that a profitable whale fishery might
be established on the shores of Fernando Po.

Mr. Laird, in his remarks on our commerce with
Africa, observes, " My proposal is, to make the government's head quarters at Fernando Po, which, from
its geographical position, is the key to central Africa,
and within a few miles of the great seats of our present commerce on the coast. It is also the only
place upon the whole line of coast, on which hospitals
and other conveniences could be erected, far above
the reach of the coast fever, where invalids from the
naval, military, and civil establishments, from all

parts of the coast, might recruit their health in a
pure and bracing atmosphere."*

Fernando Po therefore, in every way, and in a very
remarkable manner, possesses those advantages of
which we stand in need.   Is it our object to capture
the slave-trader?   Here is an island adjacent to his
chief resort, so situated as to command and control
the whole Bights of Benin and Biafra.   Or is it
our object to encourage legitimate commerce?   Fernando Po is at the outlet of that great stream which
offers a highway into the heart of Africa.   I confess, I look forward to the day, when Africa shall
unfold her hidden treasures to the world; and as a
primary means of enabling her to do so, this island
is of incalculable value.   Do we dread the climate?
Here, and as I believe, almost here alone, on the
western coast of Africa, has nature provided a position, which enjoys the benefit of perpetual sea-
breezes, free from the noxious effluvia which load
even these breezes as we advance inland on the continent; whilst its high land is above " the fatal fever
level."   Or is it our object, as far as possible, to
reduce the sufferings, and spare the lives of the
negroes, whom we, with the most generous intentions,
rescue from the slave-trader?   Under the present
system, we consign these negroes in vast numbers to
destruction, consequent on a five weeks' voyage to
Sierra Leone, when they could be landed on the

* Laird, vol. ii. p. 391.

island of Fernando Po, within a few hours, or, at most, within a few days, after their capture; while, if located on that island, they would afford material for the formation of what may be termed a normal school, for the introduction of agriculture, civilization, and Christianity into the interior of Africa.

To the reader who may be desirous of obtaining further information respecting this island, I strongly recommend the perusal of the abstract of a letter which I insert in the Appendix.*   It was written, as its date (Sept. 1835) proves, without reference to the plans which I now propose, and it did not come into my possession, till after the above description of the island had been prepared.   It will be seen, however, how remarkably it confirms the statements I have made on other authorities.

Next in importance to Fernando Po, is a settlement at the confluence of the Niger and the Tchadda.   It can hardly be doubted, I think, even by those who are most sceptical with regard to predictions of future commercial greatness, that this position will, hereafter, become the great internal citadel of Africa, and the great emporium of her commerce.   It commands the Niger, with all its tributary streams and branches in the interior, while Fernando Po exercises the same control over its numerous mouths.   With these two positions, and with our steamers plying between them, it is not too much to say, that this great river would

* *Vide* Appendix B.

be safe from the ravages of the pirate and the man-hunter, and would be open to the capital and enterprise of the legitimate merchant. I must here avail myself of a passage from a work published nearly twenty years ago :—*

"The extent of country and population whose improvements, labours, and wants would be dependent upon, and stimulated to exertions by a settlement on the Niger, is prodigious, and altogether unequalled. The extent comprehends a country of nearly 40° of longitude from west to east, and through the greater part of this extent of 20° of latitude from north to south, a space almost equal to Europe. Where the confluence of the Tschadda with the Niger takes place, is the spot to erect the capital of our great African establishments. A city built there, under the protecting wings of Great Britain, would ere long become the capital of Africa. Fifty millions of people, yea, even a greater number, would be dependant on it.

*   *   *   *

"The rivers are the roads in the torrid zone. Nature seems to have intended these as the great help in introducing agriculture and commerce.

* The "View of Northern Central Africa" was published before it was known that the Niger emptied itself into the Bight of Benin, and when the prevailing theories gave that river an opposite direction. The author, Mr. M'Queen, is at least entitled to the credit of having clearly pointed out its true course; all that he then asserted has been verified by the expedition of Laird and Oldfield.

" Wherever the continents are most extensive, there we find the most magnificent rivers flowing through them, opening up a communication from side to side. What is still more remarkable, and becomes of great utility, is, that these mighty currents flow against the prevailing winds, thus rendering the navigation easy, which would otherwise be extremely tedious and difficult. The prevailing trade-winds blow right up their streams. This is the case with the Niger, and in a more particular manner during the time it is in flood. For ten months in the year, but more particularly from May till November, the prevailing wind in the Bights of Benin and Biafra is from south-west, thus blowing right up all the outlets of the Niger. In the Congo, Tuckey found the breeze generally blowing up the stream. It is needless to point out, at length, the advantages which may be derived from this wise regulation in the natural world."

I have dwelt thus much on the Niger and the settlements connected with it, because it clearly holds the foremost place among the great inlets to Africa; but the number and situation of many other navigable rivers on the western coast of Africa have been much remarked by those who have visited them, as affording the noblest means for extending the commerce of this country to the millions who dwell on their banks, or occupy the cities and towns in the interior. Along the coast, commencing at the southern

point of the Bight of Biafra, and embracing the coast
of Calabar, the Slave Coast, the Gold Coast, the
Ivory Coast, the Grain Coast, the Pepper Coast, the
coast of Sierra Leone, and thence northwards to the
Senegal, there cannot be less than ninety or one
hundred rivers, many of them navigable, and two of
them rivalling in their volume of water and extent
the splendid rivers of North America. It is reported
that a French steam-vessel plies more than 700 miles
up the Senegal, and that the Faleme, which flows
into it eight leagues below Galam, is navigable in
the rainy season for vessels of sixty tons burden.
The Faleme runs through the golden land of Bambouk, whence the French traders obtain considerable
quantities of that precious metal. The Gambia is a
noble river. It is about eleven miles wide at its
mouth, and about four opposite Bathurst. How far
it extends into the interior is unknown; it is said,
however, that it has been ascended for some hundred
miles.* It is also asserted that from the upper part
of this river the Senegal can be reached in three, and
the Niger in four days.

In addition to the mighty rivers above referred to,

* In 1834, Captain Quin carried Governor Rendall up to
Macarthy's Island, in the Britomart sloop of war. Craft of 50
or 60 tons can get up to Fattatenda, the resort of caravans for
trade with British merchants. Commodore Owen terms the
Gambia " a magnificent river." It was surveyed in 1826 by
Lieutenant Owen, R.N., on which occasion he was accompanied
by the Acting Governor Macaulay, as far as Macarthy's Island,
180 miles up the river.—*Owen*, ii

it has been ascertained that, from Rio Lagos to the river Elrei, no fewer than twenty streams enter the ocean, several of surprising magnitude, and navigable for ships (M'Queen) ; and that all the streams which fall into the sea from Rio Formosa to Old Calabar inclusive, are connected together by intermediate streams, at no great distance from the sea.

The geographical position of Africa, and its contiguity to Europe claim for it especial attention. The voyage from the port of London to the Senegal is generally accomplished in twenty-five days; to the Gambia in twenty-eight or thirty days; to Sierra Leone, in thirty to thirty-five days; to Cape Coast Castle, in forty-two to forty-eight days; to Fernando Po, forty-eight to fifty-three days; to the ports in the Bight of Biafra, in fifty to fifty-five days; to the Zaire or Congo, in fifty-five to sixty days, respectively. Vessels leaving Bristol or Liverpool for the same ports possess an advantage, in point of time, of from five to eight days. The voyage is attended with little danger, provided common care be used. The homeward voyage is of course considerably longer than the outward, in consequence of the vessels being obliged to take what is commonly called, the western passage, having generally to go as far as 40° west longitude. The difference in the length of the voyages, outward and homeward, may be stated at from three to four weeks.

The use of steam would, of course, greatly diminish

the length of the voyage, and facilitate the operations of the trader, until establishments could be formed to which the produce required might be conveyed by the natives.

The best season for visiting the African coast is the *dry* season, that is, from December to May. But it may be remarked that the line of coast from Cape Palmas to Cape St. Paul's is less subject to rains than the Windward Coast or the Bights, and may be visited at any season. The worst period of the year is from the middle of July to the middle of December.*

With regard to commerce, then, this portion of Africa would have fair play : her resources may prove greater, or less than we suppose ; but, whatever they be, the traffic arising from them will possess that first and indispensable requisite—security.

I do not, however, anticipate that this commerce will in the first instance be large. Africa is only capable of producing : as yet, she does not produce. When it is found that there is security for person and

* The chief causes of the sickness and mortality on board trading vessels may be ascribed, first, to climate ; second, to overwork, and especially exposure to the action of the sun while working ; and, third, to drunkenness. This last is the chief cause of mortality. One great means of preventing sickness would be, to make it imperative for all trading-vessels to employ a certain number of natives, as is done on board men-of-war.

Mr. Becroft (a merchant who resided for a number of years at Fernando Po) went up the Niger in the Quorra steam-boat, on a trading voyage, in 1836 ; his expedition lasted three months. He had with him a crew of forty persons, including five white men. Only one individual died, a white man, who was previously far gone in consumption.

property, and that products of industry find a ready market, and command a supply of European articles which the natives covet, an impulse will, no doubt, be given to internal cultivation.   But it is greatly to be desired, that this impulse should be as strong, and operate as speedily, as possible. What we want is, to supplant the Slave Trade by another trade, which shall be more lucrative.   We cannot expect that savage nations will be greatly influenced by the promise of prospective advantage.   The rise of the legitimate trade ought, if we are to carry the good-will of the natives along with us, to follow as close as possible upon the downfall of the trade in man : there ought to be an immediate substitute for the gains which are to cease.   In short, the natives must be assisted, and by every method in our power put in the way of producing those things which will bear a value in the market of the world.   It is impossible that we can be in error in assuming that Africa, under cultivation, will make more from her exports than she now receives from the sale of her population.

There is no danger that the experiment will fail, if time enough is allowed for the full development of its results : but there is very considerable risk that the experiment while advancing to maturity will fail, from the impatience of a barbarous people, who are not in the habit of contemplating distant results, and who, finding themselves stripped of one species of customary trade, have not as yet been remunerated by the acquisition of a better source of revenue. For this reason, I have already suggested that we should, for a time, subsidize the chiefs of Africa, whose assistance we require; and, for the same reason, I now propose that we should give all natural, and even some artificial stimulants to agricultural industry.

If at the moment when the African population find themselves in unaccustomed security, and feel, for the first time, a certainty of reaping what they sow; when they see their river, which has hitherto been worse than useless to the bulk of the people—(for it has brought on its waves only an armed banditti, and carried away from their smouldering villages only that banditti exulting in their captured prey)—transformed into the cheapest, the safest, and the most convenient highway between themselves, and the civilized world, and discover it to be the choicest blessing which nature has bestowed upon them; if at the moment when a market is brought to their doors, and foreign merchants are at hand, ready to exchange for their productions the alluring articles of European manufacture, of which, sparingly as they have hitherto tasted, they know the rare beauty, and surpassing usefulness,—if at this moment, when so many specific and powerful motives invite them to the diligent cultivation of their soil, they are visited by a band of agricultural instructors, who offer at once to put them in possession of that skill in husbandry which the rest of the world has acquired, and they are enabled to till their ground in security, and find opened to them a conveyance for its productions, and a market for their sale; and if simultaneously with these advantages we furnish that practical knowledge, and those mechanical contrivances which the experience of ages, and the ingenuity of successive generations, have by slow degrees disclosed to ourselves—I cannot doubt that those combined benefits and discoveries will furnish an immediate, as well as an ample compensation for the loss of that wicked traffic, which, if it has afforded profit to the few, has exposed the great mass of the inhabitants to unutterable wretchedness.

CHAPTER IV.

RESULTS OF EXPERIENCE.

AFRICA, it is true, is in great measure untried
ground, yet there is some information to be derived
from the history of those colonies, few and imperfect
though they be, which have been attempted along her
coasts. There are also important hints to be found
in the recorded opinions (many of them drawn from
actual experiment) of those who are best acquainted
with the subject, whether government officers, travellers, or others. It may now be convenient to turn
our attention to the colonies which already belong
to us in Africa : in the history of them there is much
to confirm my views. I extract the following passage
from a paper written by Mr. Bandinel, dated Foreign
Office, March 30, 1839 :—

" So long ago as in 1792, the colony of Sierra
Leone was founded by benevolent individuals, for the
express purpose of inducing the natives to abandon
the traffic. The course taken was two-fold :—the
one, to educate the natives, with the view of teaching
them to give up the Slave Trade, on a religious principle ; the other, to substitute for that trade a more
legitimate commerce.

" The accounts, soon after the settlement was
formed, stated, that the natives crowded round the
colony both for education and for trade ; and that the

beneficial effect on them, in inducing them to quit
Slave-trading, was instantaneous. That effect has
been continued, and has extended, in the neighbourhood of Sierra Leone, to a very considerable distance
round the colony. Traders bring down the ivory, the
gold-dust, and palm-oil, as usual. Of late years, a
very important branch has been added to the legal
trade, by the cutting of timber for the British navy ;
and the minds of the natives are thus effectually di-
verted from the baneful occupation of the Slave
Trade, to the pursuits of legitimate commerce."

I admit, that Sierra Leone has failed to realize all
the expectations which were at one time indulged.
It must, I fear, be confessed, that the situation was
ill-chosen,—the north-west wind blows on it from
the Bulloom shore, covered with mangrove-swamps,
which generate the most destructive malaria. The
district is small, by no means affording space for a
fair experiment of our system. Nor is the land of
the peninsula well suited for the growth of tropical
productions; and there is wanting that, without which
we can hardly expect to see commerce spring up and
thrive in a barbarous country,—a river navigable far
into the interior. Besides these natural difficulties,
there have been some, arising from the system which
we have adopted, or " rather," in the words of one of
the strongest advocates in favour of Sierra Leone, " in
the want of anything like system or preconcerted plan
in the administration of its government . . . the whole
of its administration, with the exception of its judicial

system, was left to the chapter of accidents. No instructions were sent from home ; every governor was left to follow the suggestions of his own mind, both as regarded the disposal and treatment of the liberated Africans, and the general interests of the colony. . . . . . Every governor has been left to follow his own plans, however crude and undigested ; and no two succeeding governors have ever pursued the same course. This remark applies more particularly to the management of the liberated Africans."

I find this view confirmed in the third Resolution of the Report of the Select Committee on the State of Sierra Leone, 1830, which runs thus :—" It is the opinion of this Committee, that the progress of the liberated Africans in moral and industrious habits has been greatly retarded by the frequent change of system in their location and maintenance, and by the yearly influx of thousands of their rude and uncivilized countrymen."

This resolution notices another peculiarity in the case of Sierra Leone, which ought always to be borne in mind when it is brought forward as an instance of what may be done in African colonies. This peculiarity consists in the nature of its population, " a heterogeneous mass," but mainly composed of the surviving cargoes of captured slave-ships,—men who have undergone a great shock,—uprooted beings,— compelled colonists of a strange land. In addition to this original disadvantage, there have undoubtedly been great errors and omissions in the management of them. According to Colonel Denham, superintendant of that department, there has been " the want of instruction, capital, and example ;" yet he adds, "with the very little they have had of either, conveyed in a manner likely to benefit them generally, it is to me daily an increasing subject of astonishment, that the liberated Africans settled here have done so much for themselves as they have."

Sierra Leone has unquestionably laboured under very great disadvantages.* But, with all its defects, if anything has anywhere been done for the benefit of Western Africa, it has been there. The only glimmer of civilization ; the only attempt at legitimate commerce ; the only prosecution, however faint, of agriculture, are to be found at Sierra Leone, and at some of those settlements which I have just named. And there alone the Slave Trade has been in any degree arrested. We may regret, therefore, that the experiment was not tried under more favourable circumstances, on a more healthy spot, on a more

* I have compared various and conflicting accounts of Sierra Leone ; the Reports of the Company, and of the African Institution ; the able Reports of Colonel Denham on the Liberated Africans, and other Government Despatches ; the Statements of Mr. M'Queen, and the Reply of Mr. Kenneth Macaulay ; and the Evidence before both the Aborigines Committees, and that on the state of Sierra Leone, together with several private letters of authority ; and I believe my statements will all be found accurate, though my authorities are too voluminous, and too varied, to quote or extract at length.

fertile and suitable soil, on a larger scale, less exposed to the inroads of the slave-trader, and in the vicinity of one of the great arteries of Africa. Still, experience speaks strongly in its favour, because many thousands of human beings, taken from the holds of slave-ships, and placed there in the rudest state of barbarism, have made considerable advances in civilization,* because thousands of Negro children have re-

---

* Captain Ramsay told me that he had been particularly struck with the intelligent conversation and refined manners of a person in whose company he dined at Fernando Po, and whom he thought capable of filling almost any situation. Had it not been for his complexion, he would have supposed that he had been educated in England. This man was brought thither, not many years before, in the hold of a slave-ship. Mr. H. W. Macaulay, Commissary Judge at Sierra Leone, stated before a Parliamentary Committee, in 1837, that a large portion of these people, brought, as they have been, to the " colony in a savage state," landed, as he has seen many thousands of them, in a diseased and wretched condition, yet become civilized and useful members of society. He states, that these men form the militia : they serve not only as constables and attendants on the Courts of Justice, but also as jurymen ; and they discharge this duty so satisfactorily, that Mr. Macaulay further states, that, having himself had questions of large amount before them, he should at all times be willing to abide by their verdict. In speaking of the advancement to which these people have attained, he says : " There are many such instances of liberated Africans : one in particular, which I recollect, where a man, who not very long since was in the hold of a slave-ship, is acquiring at present an income of, I suppose, from 1,200*l.* to 1,500*l.* a-year. He has the government contracts for the supply of beef to the army and navy, and has had them for many years past, and he has always fulfilled his contracts to the satisfaction of

ceived and are receiving the rudiments of Christian education, and because a trade has there taken root, in itself inconsiderable enough, it is true, but yet, *one-third of the whole legitimate trade* of Central Africa. The very fact, that so large a proportion of African commerce has taken refuge, as it were, in a spot so inconvenient, while none is found on that mighty river which flows from the centre of Africa into the Atlantic, is in itself, to my apprehension, an unanswerable and authoritative proof, that, could the system of protection and instruction be tried on right principles, and upon a large scale, we need not despair of witnessing a great and glorious change in the condition of that continent.

Since the above remarks were written, I have received a letter from Mr. Ferguson, a gentleman of great intelligence and experience, who was originally sent out to Sierra Leone under the auspices of the African Institution, and is now, and has been for the last eight years, at the head of the medical department there. The document is so interesting, and so highly important, that I have ventured to quote it at considerable length; not, however, without having, in parts, curtailed the original paper, as it respects a few facts and statements of minor importance :—

" Having resided at Sierra Leone during a period of seventeen years, and had many opportunities of

the Government. He is living in a very excellent house ; has every comfort about him ; and has educated two of his children in England."

intercourse with the nations in the neighbourhood of that colony, my views of the practicability of the measures you contemplate have reference chiefly to the Windward Coast, and in a more especial manner to the colony of Sierra Leone, and to the nations immediately adjacent.

" Though the friends of Sierra Leone have long ceased to look for, or to expect any great advantage to the cause of African civilization from that quarter, I entertain a rather confident hope of being able to show that the cause is by no means so hopeless as it is generally supposed to be ; but on the contrary, that it is precisely in that quarter, and in its neighbour-hood, and at the present time, that the objects you contemplate are likely to be most speedily, and for some years at least, most extensively accomplished.

" Much money as well as much parental care and encouragement were lavished on the infant colony of Sierra Leone; but matters were so mismanaged in the outset of the undertaking, especially in the breach of faith with the Nova Scotian settlers, refusing to allot to them the quantities of land for which they had previously stipulated, that distrust and dis-content, neglect of agriculture, and inveterate habits of idleness, became general.

" After a lapse of some years, an accession was made to the colony of numbers, but by no means of moral strength, in a body of Maroons, who were sent from Jamaica after the Maroon war. They had been for many years the only body of free blacks in

the island of Jamaica. Indolent, and averse to
agriculture in their native land, their habits were by
no means changed by the transatlantic voyage, nor
have they, in fact, studied to acquire habits of industry
until this day. Thus agriculture and the useful arts
received no aid whatever from such elements as the
Sierra Leone Company had as yet employed in
furtherance of their benevolent designs.

" The abolition of the Slave Trade by Great
Britain, and its subsequently declared illegality,
under certain circumstances, by the governments of
Spain and Portugal, and the consequent capture of
vessels taken in the prosecution of the illicit trade,
introduced, in the body of liberated Africans, a third
element in the population of the colony, and it is to
the working of that third element—what it has
already done, is doing, and what may be prospectively
and reasonably expected from it, that I desire especially to direct your attention.

" The condition of a body of captured slaves on
their arrival at Sierra Leone for liberation, is the
most miserable and wretched that can be conceived—
emaciated, squalid, sickly-looking, ill-fed, barbarous,
confined in inadequate space, compelled to breathe an
atmosphere hardly fit for the sustenance of animal
life—is it to be wondered, that, in such circumstances,
the faculties of the soul should be cramped and
benumbed by the cruelties inflicted upon the body ?
It is nevertheless from among such people and their
descendants at Sierra Leone, their minds at length

elevated by a sense of personal freedom, and by the temperate administration of just and equitable laws, that you are to look for the first practical results of your operations. It is not my intention to trace the progress of the liberated Africans from the depths of misery alluded to, until we find them, after the lapse of fifteen or twenty years, independent and respectable members of society, but to give you some notion of them as a class, and of the position in society which they occupy at the present day.

" Those most recently arrived are to be found occupying mud houses and small patches of ground in the neighbourhood of one or other of the villages, which are about twenty in number. The majority of these remain in their location as agriculturists; but several go to reside in the neighbourhood of Freetown as labourers, farm servants, servants to carry wood and water, grooms, house servants, &c. Others cultivate vegetables, rear poultry and pigs, or offer for sale a variety of edible substances. They are a harmless and well disposed people; there is no poverty nor begging amongst them; their habits are frugal and industrious, and their anxiety to possess money remarkable.

" Persons of a grade higher than those just described are to be found occupying frame houses, and are mostly employed either in carrying on small trades in the market, in buying and retailing the cargoes of native canoes, in curing and drying fish, or in working at various mechanical trades. Re-

spectable men of this grade meet with ready mercantile credits, amounting from £20 to £60; and the
class is very numerous.

" Those who have advanced another step are found
in frame houses, reared on a stone foundation, of from
six to ten feet in height. These houses are very comfortable; a considerable quantity of furniture of
European workmanship, and of books, chiefly of a
religious character, is to be found in them, and an
air of domestic comfort pervading the whole. Persons of this class are nearly altogether occupied in
shopkeeping, and may be seen clubbing together in
numbers from three to six, seven, or more, to purchase
large lots or unbroken bales; and the scrupulous
honesty with which the subdivision of the goods is
afterwards made, cannot be evidenced more thoroughly
than in this, that, common as such transactions are,
they have never yet been known to become the subject of controversy or litigation. The principal
streets of Freetown, as well as the approaches to the
town, are lined on each side by an almost continuous
range of booths and stalls, among which almost every
article of merchandise is offered for sale. They are
all in easy circumstances, and are invariably anxious
to possess houses and lands of their own, especially
in Old Freetown. Property of this description has
of late years become much enhanced, and is still
increasing in value, solely from their annually
increasing numbers and prosperity.

" Persons of the highest grade of liberated Africans

occupy comfortable two-story stone houses, inclosed all round with spacious piazzas. These houses are their own property, and are built from the proceeds of their own industry. In several of them are to be seen mahogany chairs, tables, sofas, and four-post bedsteads, pier glasses, floor cloths, and other articles indicative of domestic comfort and accumulating wealth. They are almost wholly engaged in mercantile pursuits, and are to be found in neatly fitted-up shops on the ground-floor of their respective dwelling-houses. Many of them have realized considerable sums of money. Peter Newland, a liberated African, died a short time before I left the colony, and his estate realized, in houses, merchandise, and cash, upwards of £1,500. I am well acquainted with one of these individuals, whose name, shortly before my departure from the colony, stood on the debtor side of the books of one of the principal merchants for £1,900, to which sum it had been reduced from £3,000 during the preceding two months. Many of them at the present moment have their children being educated in England at their own expense.

"There is at Sierra Leone a very fine regiment of colonial militia, more than eight-tenths of which are liberated Africans. The amount of property which they have acquired is ample guarantee for their loyalty, should that ever be called in question. They turn out with great alacrity and cheerfulness on all occasions for periodical drill. They also serve on juries; and I have repeatedly heard the highest legal authority in the colony express his satisfaction with their decisions.

" From the preceding details it may be inferred, that a leading feature in the character of the liberated Africans is their great love of money. But this, though remarkable, is by no means of that sordid nature which induces the miser to hoard up his wealth for its own sake. On the contrary, their whole surplus means are devoted to the increase of their domestic comforts and the improvement of their outward appearance of respectability A comfortable house is the first great object of their desire. For this they are content to labour at any sort of work, and turn themselves diligently and cheerfully to any honest means of earning money. The working hours are from six in the morning till four in the afternoon, with one hour of interval for breakfast. Labour is to be had in abundance at 4*d*. per diem. Very needy persons may sometimes be found who will work for 3½*d*. A good overseer or headsman may be had at 5*d*. per diem, or 13*s*. per month.

" Of the liberated Africans as a body, it may with great truth be said that there is not a more quiet, inoffensive, and good humoured population on the face of the earth. Of their religious spirit it is not easy, from the very nature of the subject, to form a decided opinion, but I know that their outward observance of the Sabbath-day is most exemplary. On that day the passion for amusements is altogether laid aside, and the whole body of the people are to be found at one or other of the churches or chapels, which abound in the colony.

" It may be presumed, from what has been said of their love of gain, that in their habits and desires they are decidedly industrious. But, however successful, from the abundance of European example, they may have been in the application of their energies and industry to pursuits of a mercantile nature, it is to be regretted that no similar example in the department of agriculture has as yet been placed before them. Were such example afforded in the culture of such articles as would at all times meet with a ready purchaser, I am warranted in averring, with much confidence, that energies similar to those which (as we have already seen) have been so zealously and successfully directed to trade, would promptly, and with equal zeal, be found engaged in agriculture. In 1826 Mr. Clouston, a respectable merchant of Freetown, planted a small quantity of ginger by way of experiment, and having reported favourably of it, its culture was immediately taken up by a vast body of liberated Africans. Ignorance was, however, displayed at every step of their progress. They planted indiscriminately in sterile and in rich soils, so that the sample produced was a mixture of plump and meagre roots. By some the sample was dried previously to being offered for sale, by others not; by some it was carefully cleaned, which others neglected; so that the merchants became averse to purchase it, and the growers saw their hopes blighted. In 1829 their attention was turned to the culture of capsicum, by the sale of a lot at Freetown, which fetched 2*s*. 6*d*. per pound. It would have been difficult at that time to have collected two tons of pepper in the colony, but in the course of a very few years individual merchants were found exporting 100 and 150 tons per annum. The price however, fell to 4*d*. per pound; sales could not even then be effected; and the hopes of the cultivators were again disappointed. In 1833 their expectations were similarly raised and blighted by the encouragement held out for the manufacture of cassada starch. Instances might be multiplied, but I think those just noted are sufficient to show that the liberated Africans are not only willing but desirous that their attention should be directed to the culture of such articles as will afford them a certain return for their labour and industry; and that the position at which they have arrived in the social state is precisely that to which the labours of philanthropists may be applied satisfactorily to themselves, and with a certain prospect of advantage to that interesting people.

" Among other circumstances indicative of the improvement of their worldly means, and of their desire still further to avail themselves of European example, none stands more prominently forward than the system which they have lately commenced of sending their children to England for education. Thirty years ago a few liberated African boys were sent to England and educated at the expense of the

African Institution, with a view to their aid in working out the general objects of the Institution at Sierra Leone. These boys, on their return to the colony, with one exception, speedily fell back on the barbarous habits of their youth, and their public utility fell far short of the expectations of their patrons. We now, however, behold under different auspices the same class of persons considerably advanced in wealth and civilization, desiring European education for their children of their own accord, without advice or pecuniary aid from others, and moved thereto solely by a conviction of its intrinsic excellence. There are now, however, but few outlets for the employment of educated young men in the colony; and it appears clear that the quantity of talent of this description which will become available will in a short time far exceed the means of employment. The present is therefore precisely the time for the friends of African civilization to adopt such measures as may appear best calculated to secure the effectual co-operation of the new element which is about to be placed before them.

" Several articles of tropical agriculture have been from time to time tried at Sierra Leone on a small scale, and the experiments have been generally successful. The most decided, as well as the most carefully performed and most successful of these, was the introduction, a few years ago, by some of the gentlemen of the Church Missionary Society, of some of the seeds of the Sea-island cotton. I have stated above,

that were examples in agriculture offered as liberally
as they have been in trade, the former would be followed up by the liberated Africans with as much
diligence and zeal as they have been found to have
devoted to the latter. It would, however, be important, in conducting such an experiment, that their
attention should, in the first instance, be directed to
such articles as in their culture require the smallest
outlay of money, the shortest time to bring them to
maturity, and a sure sale whenever and in whatever
quantity they may be brought to market.

" No article seems to afford these requisites with
such a prospect of certainty as cotton ; and a normal
farm of 100 acres, for the culture of that article, in
the south-eastern part of the colony, would, I am
well assured, be followed within two years by a general rush of the whole agricultural population
towards its production. The actual sight of a considerable quantity grown in the colony, offered for
sale, and immediately purchased, would render
any further experimental effort in regard to that
article useless ; except, indeed, in respect of the
best kind of seed to be used, and the most approved
mode of culture.

" But this is, perhaps, the smallest amount of benefit that would ensue. The natives of the countries in
the immediate vicinity of Sierra Leone take a large
quantity of British manufactures in return for African teak, the cutting and squaring of which is
nearly altogether performed by slave labour. The

sort of traffic to which it has given rise, has, nevertheless, so clearly demonstrated to the native chiefs
how much more advantageous it is to work their
slaves than to sell them, that Slave Trading (I mean
the selling of slaves) in the countries adjacent to
Sierra Leone has nearly altogether ceased. In
some of these countries the timber is now obtained
with much more difficulty than formerly, owing to
the greater distance from the water-side at which
it has to be procured. Should this difficulty increase to such a length as to render the cutting of
timber no longer profitable, the hands left unem-
ployed in such a case would, in the culture of cotton, find ample means of profitable employment; and
by this means the continuance and permanence of
the first great step in African civilization would, to
the inhabitants of those countries, be secured. I fear
that these people are not yet so far removed from
the recollections of a flourishing Slave Trade as to
render its abandonment by them the result of sound
principle, or of a conviction of its cruelty. The continuance of the legitimate trade on which they have
already so successfully entered, may, however, in the
hands of another generation, establish its final abandonment on more reputable motives. Meantime, in
the cutting of timber, and in the growth of rice, we
have undoubted proofs of their industry, and of their
willingness, by bodily labour, to obtain what they may
require of European manufactures.

" I trust that in this sketch of the liberated

Africans, of the progress which they have already
made, and of the efforts which they are still making,
towards civilization, you will find not only sufficient
encouragement to induce you to devote towards the
colony of Sierra Leone a portion of your fostering
care ; but also that you will perceive that the present is the time when instruction and encouragement, especially in the practice of agriculture, afford
a fairer prospect of being crowned with success, than
at any other period in the previous history or condition of the colony.

" I have a moral certainty that the advances which
they have already made in knowledge and in wealth
cannot possibly be arrested at the present stage, and
that an impulse has been given to the onward course
of improvement, the limit of which, in respect to
them, is not yet in sight. But however certain their
future progress may be in the course on which they
have so auspiciously entered, it is clear that that progress might be accelerated tenfold, were there, in well
conducted examples, and in competent instruction,
as it were a beacon held out to them, teaching them
alike what to avoid and what to cling to, as well in
the mode of culture, as in the article to be cultivated.

" There are places on the Windward Coast of
Western Africa, other than Sierra Leone, which I
think would repay any care that might be bestowed
on them, in the way of agricultural instruction and
example ; and, perhaps, none will be found better

H

calculated for its application than the settlements on
the river Gambia.　The soil is rich, and more easily
brought under culture than even that of Sierra
Leone ; ground nuts and corn are grown there ; and
cotton, also, in a considerable quantity, and of a texture which, as I have been informed by respectable
merchants, equals much that is brought from the
West Indies and South America, although their
mode of preparing it is inferior.　At the extensive
Government farm near Bathurst, which is worked by
liberated Africans, such quantities of ground nuts
and corn are raised, as far more than pay all the expenses of management ; and were example and the
necessary instruction afforded, the culture of cotton
might there be substituted with great advantage, and
at no additional expense.

　" Keeping steadily in sight your principle of substituting a harmless and profitable trade for one that
is illegal and worse than profitless, I am also desirous
of directing your attention to what has been going on
during the last year or two in the Rio Nunez.　This
river, though now little spoken of, was in former
years notorious for Slave Trading.

　" At Kaikandy, the chief trading place, situated
about 100 miles from the sea, and in the country of
the Landemas, numerous factories, occupied by
French and English traders, are established ; to
which Foulahs, Seracoolies, Bambarras, and people
of other nations, resort in great numbers.　I spent
some time there in February last, and was assured

by the merchants that the Foulahs were gradually weaning themselves from the Slave Trade, and that they had of late years brought down a much larger quantity of native produce than formerly; an assurance which was confirmed as well by the number of English and French merchants established there in the prosecution of legitimate commerce, as by the *single slave-trader,* Señor Caravalho, a Portuguese.

" About three years ago, some of the Foulah traders who resort to Kaikandy, brought down small parcels of coffee, and offered them for sale. The coffee was so eagerly purchased by the European merchants, that the Foulahs immediately turned their attention to the further supply of it. It appears that there are vast forests of indigenous coffee in the Foulah country, and of much finer quality than that of the West Indies or South America. The Foulahs evince great satisfaction in the possession of such an unexpected source of wealth, and the quantity supplied has of course greatly increased; but, unfortunately, this infant trade, at the very dawning of its existence, is threatened with destruction; it being found that the protective duty for British plantation was so high as to prove tantamount to a total exclusion of the Foulah coffee, the duty on the former being 6*d*., and on the latter 1*s.* 3*d.*, per pound. The merchants at Kaikandy have, nevertheless, continued to purchase the coffee, in whatever quantities it has been offered, in the hope that the British Government may yet be disposed to relieve them of their difficulties.

"But the most grievous part of the disappointment is, that it would be difficult to devise any mode calculated more powerfully and effectually to disenthral the people from the desire of kidnapping and selling each other, than the admission of the Foulah coffee into the ports of Great Britain on terms similar to those of British plantation.

"You will perceive from this detail, that the Foulahs, without any extrinsic aid, have already done much in furthering the object you have at heart; that they want assistance; that the present is the time at which that assistance may most effectually be applied; and also the nature of the assistance required.

"The Foulahs are an intelligent people, and are very anxious to extend their commercial dealings with the British. They seem to have already perceived that it is more profitable for them to preserve the element of labour in their own country, than to deprive themselves of its assistance by selling each other to strangers; so that it may be said, without a metaphor, that in every hundred-weight of coffee which they collect and take to Kaikandy, at least one human being is preserved from slavery.

"An instance illustrative of their desire to preserve and extend their commercial relations with the British occurred a few months ago. A temporary

interruption was thrown in the way of both the export
and import trade of the river (Nunez), by certain
dissensions among the tributary chiefs, the continuance of which was likely to prove highly detrimental
to the interests of the British and other merchants
established at Kaikandy. Lieutenant Hill, of her
Majesty's brig Saracen, on being made acquainted
with the danger to which British property was exposed, very promptly set sail for the Rio Nunez for
its protection.   On his arrival there, a grand palaver
was called, for the purposes of investigating the
causes of this disturbance, and of restoring tranquillity. The conference which ensued was presided over
by a Foulah chief, who appeared to be established at
Kaikandy in an official character, and to be clothed
with functions (as the event showed) of a nature more
full and extensive than those of a mere consul or
chargé d'affaires.

" It appeared by the majority of voices, and by an
almost unanimous concurrence of opinion, that the
cause and continuance of the disturbances were attri-
butable to the intrigues of a Mandingo named Boi
Modao.

" The Foulah chief addressed himself to Lieut.
Hill, in a speech explanatory of the great anxiety of
the Foulah king to maintain and to extend commercial intercourse with the British, and his determina-
tion to put down and remove any obstacle to its continuance that should arise ; and to satisfy Lieut. Hill

of the sincerity of his professions, he offered then and there to decapitate Boi Modao, and thus at once restore trade to its usual channels. Lieut. Hill, of course, declined a proof of sincerity so unequivocal and convincing.

" The conference was no sooner at an end than Boi Modao, with marks of great haste and much alarm, fled from that part of the country, and trade was carried on as usual."

We now proceed to the further consideration of the Gambia. " In the year 1814," says Mr. Bandinel, " a colony was formed at St. Mary's, on the river Gambia, by British settlers, who removed from the coasts of Senegal, when it was restored to the French. This colony has increased and flourished beyond all reasonable calculation, and is already more powerful and wealthy than any of those elder settlements of the British in Africa, which were formed for the purpose of promoting the Slave Trade·

" The beneficial effects of the settlement of St. Mary's, on all the tribes along the banks of the Gambia, are perhaps still more prominent than those which have taken place round Sierra Leone."

" The Gambia was formerly a great mart for slaves. The population along its banks are now eager for lawful commerce, in which alone they are now engaged. The trade is extended above 400 miles up the river ; a new and lucrative branch has also been lately opened there in gum ; and the only exception

to the cheering picture occurs in the French
establishment at Albreda, where still some slaves
are said to be harboured, obtained from natives
in the interior, and sent overland afterwards to
Goree."

The Slave Trade is, however, so small and so
declining at Albreda, that the exception may be
almost said to prove the rule ; because it shows, that
though an European establishment exists, ready to
trade in slaves, it does not flourish against the rivalry
of a legal commerce.

In the year 1833, a mission, in connexion with the
Wesleyan Society, was established at Macarthy's
Island on the Gambia, with the view of promoting
the civilization of the neighbouring tribes of Foulahs
through the medium of Christianity. To the missionaries connected with this establishment I am in-
debted for much valuable information respecting the
present state of Western Africa. The Rev. R. M.
Macbrair, in a M.S. statement with which he has
favoured me, ascribes the abolition of the Slave
Trade in the neighbourhood of the Gambia to two
causes; first, to the vicinity of the British colony,
and its command over the river ; and, secondly, to
the existence of a good market for the produce of
the soil. The change effected by these circumstances Mr. Macbrair thus describes :—" Culture
is more practised in the neighbourhood of the Gambia, where affairs are now comparatively peaceful.
Before the abolition of the Slave Trade, there were

considerable factories here; and one native merchant,
now at St. Mary's, was sold no less than three times
by another, who resides in the same place. One of
the kings also, is said to have "seized and disposed of
some of his subjects whenever he wanted a horse, a
wife, or other purchasable commodity." But now
that the slave-market is abolished, and the natives
can find a ready market for the produce of their
lands by means of the British merchants, the cultivation of the soil increases every year; and the Aborigines have been heard to say, that they now wish
they had their slaves back again, because they could
get more by their labours in husbandry, than they
did by selling them to Europeans."

Mr. Finden, who has been a resident merchant on
the Gambia for the last 17 years, says, in a letter to
me, dated 4th May, 1838—" Prior to the formation
of the settlement, the trade consisted almost wholly
in slaves; and vessels, fitted out for the purpose, proceeded up the river about 300 miles. Since that
period, I can state from correct information, and my
own knowledge, that no slaves have been exported
in any vessel from the Gambia; and in lieu of this
horrible traffic, a valuable and legitimate commerce has been established there, which by encouragement might be considerably increased and
rendered most valuable to the mother country."
" This," he thinks, "might be effected by extending protection, at least as high up the river as it is
navigable in the dry season. I should consider

Fattatenda* and Kantally Coonda the most desirable
spots. By this means, greater quantities of our
exports could be thrown into the country, and trade
drawn from a much greater distance, and we should
thus be enabled, in a great measure, to check the
slave-traders who pass these places on their way to
the different leeward slave-depôts. An armed steam-
vessel would be of great service, and would afford
a protection to trading vessels and factories established on the banks of the river, which are at present rendered unsafe by the depredations committed
by marauding chiefs."

These views are fully concurred in by the Rev.
John Morgan, to whose zeal the Foulah mission
partly owes its origin. He recommends the purchase
of tracts of land adjoining the principal rivers which
flow into the Atlantic, in which the natives might
find security from the predatory incursions of the
chiefs, and from the cupidity of the slave-trader;
and he likewise suggests the employment of an armed
steam-vessel attached to each settlement. He says,
" I am convinced that thousands would flee to such
places of refuge, as soon as they could be assured of
protection, and thus a dense free population would

* A considerable trade is already carried on at the port of Fattatenda, beyond which merchant-vessels do not proceed. The
Rev. W. Fox, who visited it in 1837, describes it as " the resort
of caravans from the interior ;" and consequently a considerable
concourse of people is invariably attracted thither in the pursuit
of commerce.

soon spring up, and agriculture and commerce would rapidly extend. These settlements might soon be rendered capable of defending themselves, and a great saving of European life would be immediately effected, as the interior of the country is far more salubrious than the coast."

Here I must again express my regret that the usefulness of our principal African settlements should have been impaired by an injudicious selection of localities, and by a too contracted scale of operations. The disadvantages with which they have had to contend are thus stated by Mr. Morgan :—" Being situated on the coast, those who most needed refuge could not reach them : secondly, they have ever been so small, that it was impossible for more than a small number to provide the means of subsistence on either of them : thirdly, in several cases, protection has not been offered to those who have fled to them." To these causes, I think, it may be attributed that our success has been so limited, and that so little has been done towards the accomplishment of our main object.

We find, however, in the immediate neighbourhood of the Gambia, where the influence of the British flag is felt, the Slave Trade has been suppressed, and comparative tranquillity and security have been established. But we do not proceed far into the interior, before we meet with the same scenes of violence and rapine as before. In many cases, the slaves who were formerly brought to the mouth of the river, are now

transported over land to other parts of the coast ; the
depredations of the powerful chiefs still continue and
have hitherto rendered abortive the attempts which
have been made by the missionaries to establish native settlements on the main land, without the aid of
British protection. These circumstances confirm
me in the opinion which I have formed, in common
with those who are best acquainted with the subject,
that our settlements, in order to be effective, must be
fixed in the interior, where the Slave Trade originates,
and where our experiments can be tried at a less
costly sacrifice of human life.

I cannot conclude my notice of this colony, without
adverting to the success which has attended the labours of the missionaries, from whom I have so
largely quoted. By the latest official returns of the
establishments at St. Mary's and Macarthy's Islands,
it appears, that there are " 559 members in church
fellowship, with congregations amounting to more
than double that number." The Mandingo language,
which is generally used in that part of Western
Africa, has been reduced to grammatical form, and
translations of the gospels have been made. In the
schools, which are partly conducted by native teachers,
220 are instructed in the elements of a plain education ; and the missionaries state that they are
encouraged to persevere in their labours, by the
increasing desire manifested by the people to obtain
instruction. An interesting feature in this missionary enterprise is the experiment which is about to be

made of following up the preaching of the gospel by
instruction in the arts and pursuits of civilized life.
The site of a native village has been selected in
Macarthy's island, and 600 acres of land have been
allotted by the British government, on which some of
the Christian natives are already receiving elementary
instruction in agriculture.

The Gold Coast.

Our settlement on the Gold Coast is another
illustration of the advantage of stations in Africa.
In this case, there are two unquestionable facts,
—1st, That the Slave Trade did prevail in the
district of the Gold Coast. 2ndly, That it has
been entirely suppressed, and that a considerahle
and increasing trade has sprung up in its place.
To any one familiar with the earlier period of
the Slave Trade controversy, it will not be necessary to say, that it was perpetually referred to, as
the district which furnished by far the greater part
of the slaves taken to the British colonies. We not
only established forts there for the express purpose of
encouraging that trade, but there seems to have been
no difficulty in obtaining from parliament munificent
grants for their maintenance—30,000*l.* was the annual sum thus applied.

" These establishments," says the governor of the
colony, " constituted the great emporium whence
the British West India colonies were supplied with
slaves. Such being the case, and considering also

the vast number of slaves which were annually exported in order to meet the demands of so extensive a market, we are fully warranted in affirming, that in no part of Africa was the Slave Trade more firmly rooted, or more systematically carried on, than in these settlements."

What is now termed legitimate commerce was, previously to the passing of the Abolition Act, but little thought of, and only attended to, so far as it was auxiliary to the grand object—the acquisition of slaves. " Daily accustomed to witness scenes of the most cold-blooded cruelty, the inhabitants became utterly callous to human suffering ; each petty chieftain oppressed and plundered his weaker neighbours, to be in his turn plundered and oppressed by one stronger and more powerful than himself. In no portion of Africa, in short, was the demoralising, the brutalising influence of the Slave Trade more fearfully displayed, than in those extensive tracts of country which now form, or are adjoining to, our settlements on the Gold Coast."

But, happily, this state of things no longer exists. Within a few short years so complete a revolution has been effected, that, in the expressive words of Governor M'Lean, " *from Apollonia to Accra, not a single slave has been exported since the year* 1830."

It becomes, then, highly interesting to ascertain how, and by what means, the Slave Trade has been eradicated from a portion of Africa, comprehending a space which Governor M'Lean rates at 4000 square

miles inland, and a line of coast 180 miles in extent,
—where it had been planted, protected, fostered, and
munificently encouraged for centuries.

This great object has not been accomplished by our
naval squadrons. Her Majesty's cruisers have certainly been in the habit of visiting the settlement,
but only for the purpose of procuring supplies, and of
affording, if called upon, aid to the local authorities.
No cruiser (says the Governor) has ever, at least for
many years, been stationed off the Gold Coast for
the purpose of intercepting slaves.

This revolution has been effected by the very
agency which I desire to see tried on other parts of
the coast, and on a greater scale,—by the establishment
of a station, which, while it multiplies the difficulties and dangers of the slave-trader, will afford protection to the native in the cultivation of the soil, by
giving security to the trader, and opening a market
for the sale of the productions he rears. Crops have
been grown, and articles produced, and labour bestowed, because he who sowed knew that he should
reap, and he who laboured was no longer exposed to
the probability of seeing his acquisitions rifled, and
himself hunted after, by the marauders whom his prosperity had attracted.

It is not to be denied that there were great difficulties in the outset. The trade in man has its attractions
—it combines the hazard of the chase, with the name
and the profits of merchandize. It affords a field for the
exercise of skill—for the display of courage—for the

employment of stratagem—for the gratification of revenge. It calls forth all those martial passions, in
which savages, and others than savages, conceive that
all glory resides. To some, no doubt, it yielded wealth :
a successful sally—a fortunate adventure—a sudden
and daring surprise—rendered a profit larger than
a month's labour would produce. It was, moreover, the inveterate custom of the country. The
inhabitants knew the art of kidnapping, and knew
no other art : there seemed to them no other way
by which they could obtain those supplies of foreign
manufacture and produce, which long habit had rendered necessaries of life.

These difficulties stood in the way of the effectual
abolition of the Slave Trade : they were only to be
overcome by proving to the natives experimentally
that it was their interest to suppress it; in other words,
that they would gain by the sale of their productions
a larger amount of those foreign luxuries which they
craved, than by the sale of man. It was therefore
necessary to create some other species of traffic,
whereby the native could procure his wonted supplies.
This end could not have been effected without the
aid of resident merchants and a local government :
the one, to afford a perpetual and ready supply of the
articles which the African required, and to urge him
to provide the goods which would be taken in exchange ; the other, to protect legitimate commerce,
and to redress, and, if needful, to punish the exportation of slaves.

The experiment has been successful. The difficulties and perils which, after the Abolition law, attached to the Slave Trade, called into existence various articles of commerce previously unknown. The soil, which formerly did not yield sufficient for the sustenance of the inhabitants, now exports a very large amount of corn to Madeira ; and the natives, as we are expressly told by the governor, are better supplied with European and other merchandize than formerly, when it was the chief mart for slaves.

It does not diminish my satisfaction to know that this result was brought about by slow degrees. For many years after the Slave Trade was abolished by law, the conflict between lawful and unlawful trade continued. It was not likely that the natives would be weaned in a moment from the customs of their forefathers, or by anything short of a succession of experiments. But innocent commerce has at length fairly won the victory, and the last case which occurred is thus described. I quote it, because the narrative proves that prior to 1830, our influence had checked the Slave Trade ; and because it incidentally shows, in an official form, the customary horrors of the traffic, which, as far as the Gold Coast extends, we have been so happy as to repress.

" In the month of January, 1830, the king of Apollonia, an ally, though not a dependent on the British government, despatched messengers to Cape Coast Castle, to intimate that a Spanish slaver had

anchored off Apollonia fort, the captain of which
asserted, that he had obtained the president's leave to
purchase a cargo of slaves, and had already landed
goods for that purpose; that he (the king of Apollonia) wished to ascertain whether there was any
truth in the Spanish captain's assertion, as he
should certainly furnish him with no slaves, without the full consent and permission of the president.
The president, in reply to this message, highly
commended the conduct of the king of Apollonia, as
a reward for which he sent him a handsome present,
at the same time strictly prohibiting him from exporting, or permitting to be exported, a single slave,
and explaining to him the British laws on that
subject.

"In the mean time, the king had contrived, by
fair promises, to get into his possession the whole of
the Spanish cargo of goods; and when his messengers returned from Cape Coast Castle, he flatly refused to deliver a single slave, or return the cargo.
The Spanish captain managed, however, to get on
board his vessel several of the king's family, and intimated to him, that, unless the slaves contracted for
were furnished immediately, he would certainly carry
them (the king's hostages) off the coast; whereupon
the king, mustering his more immediate attendants
and adherents, sallied out into the town, in the night
time, and seizing all without distinction whom he
could find, sent them, to the number of 360, on board

in irons, at daybreak, receiving in return the persons detained as hostages.

" Here were 360 free people, living in their own houses, in perfect peace and apparent security, seized without the shadow of pretext, by a rapacious and remorseless tyrant, whom they had been taught to look up to as their father and protector. One of them, a Mulatto girl, about sixteen or seventeen years of age, was afterwards redeemed, and she described the consternation and horror of the poor people, when they found themselves ironed in the slaver's hold."

In a letter which I received from Governor M'Lean, dated 28th September, 1838, he again adverts to the formerly disordered state of the colony, which he thus contrasts with its present condition :—
" In 1830, all communication with Ashantee, and through it with the interior, had been entirely stopped for 10 years previously ; and the only trade done was for what gold and ivory could be procured in the districts adjoining the coast. The whole country was one scene of oppression, cruelty, and disorder ; so much so, that a trader dared not go twenty miles into the ' bush.' At present our communication with the interior is as free and safe as between England and Scotland; single messengers can, and do, travel from one end of the country to the other with perfect safety ; and no man can oppress another with impunity." Such is the important change which a local

government, with but limited resources at its command, has been enabled to effect throughout this extensive territory, in the short period of eight years,
and principally by means of a strict and impartial
administration of justice. The natives, long used to
the most cruel tyranny, warmly appreciate their present mild and equal system of government, and rely,
with perfect confidence, upon the integrity of their
rulers. The consequence is, the trade of the Gold
Coast already repays more than twenty-fold the sum
granted by Parliament for the support of the local
establishment.* Its exports to Great Britain amount
to 160,000*l.* per annum, forming one-fifth of the
whole commerce of Africa ; although the country is
by no means so fertile as many other parts of that
continent, and has not the advantage of navigable
rivers.

It is also gratifying to find that, through the labours
of the Wesleyan missionaries, Christianity is making
considerable progress in this part of Africa. The
Rev. T. B. Freeman, in a letter to the parent Society, dated 10th October, 1838, after describing in
animated terms, the prosperous state of the mission,
and the field which is now open for Christian enterprise, communicates the following interesting intelligence :—" I have received information, *viâ* Fernando Po, that several liberated Africans in the
Island of Jamaica, who are members of our Society in
the Kingston circuit, and who are natives of Cape

* United Service Journal, March, 1838.

Coast, Annamaboe, and Accra, and other places along the western coast of Africa which are under the British flag, are very anxious to return to their native land. But they are afraid of being again torn away from their homes, and exposed to all the horrors of slavery ; and, secondly, of being deprived of those Christian privileges which they now enjoy. Please to inform them that their fears are groundless ; that their persons and property will here be perfectly safe, and that several hundreds of their countrymen have embraced the truths of Christianity. They can also have employment as soon as they arrive here."

A striking contrast to the state of the Gold Coast is presented by the town of Wydah, situated on the Bight of Benin. This place is the residence of the notorious De Sousa, the slave-broker of the king of Dahomey, and it enjoys very little, if any, legitimate trade. The captain of a merchant-ship states, that he has seen there 28 slave vessels under Spanish and Brazilian colours. "These vessels," he observes, " would carry, on an average, 350 or 400 slaves each. On returning, ten months after, I have seen several of these vessels in the same roadstead, having in the interim completed a slavery voyage to Brazil and back."

To these portions of Africa, in particular, Great Britain owes a heavy debt of justice, for the many years of misery which she inflicted upon them by making them the seats of the Slave Trade ; a debt, which she can only hope to repay, by carrying out the

salutary measures which have proved so successful
in the case of the Gold Coast. But as the injury
was not limited to these localities only, so her redress
should not terminate there: in order that her compensation may be ample, and her remedy efficient,
they must be applied nearer the sources of the evil.

Our efforts, as far as they have gone, have been successful, and although our principal object has not been
attained by them, we have proved what may be effected,
by granting our protection, by encouraging commerce
and agriculture, and by diffusing the blessings of
Christianity. By adopting a similar policy in positions
more favourable, and in connexion with the other measures which I propose, I am led to believe we shall
effectually check the Slave Trade, and produce a revolution in Africa, still more signal than that which has
been already experienced in our present settlements.

It appears, then, that these three cases, Sierra
Leone, Gambia, and the Gold Coast, as far as they go,
illustrate and strengthen my views. When the errors
which have been committed in their management
shall be rectified,—when education and Christian
instruction shall prevail, and when an effective impulse shall have been given to commerce and agriculture, we, seeing what has already been done, may
reasonably hope that a salutary change will be
effected in this unhappy continent.

A further confirmation of this hope is derived from
the recorded observations of gentlemen, worthy of all

confidence, who have collected their opinions on the spot.

Governor Macarthy, in addressing the merchants of St. Mary's on the Gambia in a visit he paid them in 1818, used the following words:—" I consider the extension of an honourable trade in Africa as benefiting a considerable portion of the human race. I anticipate with delight the period when, in lieu of the horrid traffic in human life, British trade and industry will spread, and the Christian religion prevailing over Africa, the inhabitants of this vast continent will, by their emancipation from moral and physical slavery, rank among civilized nations." *

General Turner, governor of Sierra Leone, appears to have been a man of vigorous and enlarged mind : had he lived, he would probably have done much for the suppression of the Slave Trade. His reports are the more interesting to me, because I find that his views, as to the mode of accomplishing that object, closely correspond with those which I have adopted. He appears to think that the abolition is to be effected by means of treaties with the native powers; by engaging them to lend their assistance ; by thus rooting out the Slave-trader from his usual field of exertion; and by the employment of steamers on the coast: above all, by the influence of legitimate commerce.

* Nineteenth Report of Church Missionary Society.

Extracts from Despatches from Major-General Turner, late Governor of Sierra Leone.

Dated 20*th July*, 1825.

" The great increase of the Slave Trade in this neighbourhood, together with the inadequacy of the ships of war on the station, have caused me to turn my attention seriously to the evil, as well as to the remedy for it ; and whilst I admit the evil to exist to a shameful extent, I am happy to say, that I will undertake, at little or no expense, without the aid of the navy, without compromising the government, and without risk of failure, to complete in six months such arrangements as will prevent any vessel, of any nation, carrying away a cargo of slaves from Western Africa ; and I pledge myself that the completion of these measures will produce to Africa more peace and good order, more industry, prosperity, and morality, —and to England, a larger and better field for the exercise of her benevolence.

*   *   *   *

" England should prevent the *collection of these unhappy victims,* and bestow her care upon nations with knowledge to appreciate, and character to retain the advantage of an intercourse with her : that there are such nations within our reach, and that they are anxious to open a communication with us, is within my knowledge ; and that I will accomplish all these objects without much expense, if approved of, I pledge myself.   If there should be any doubt, I should beg that those who know me best may be referred to, whe-

ther I am likely to engage in wild, visionary schemes.
Should such measures be approved of, all I want
from England are two small steam-boats.

" These two boats, in addition to the one already
ordered for the general work of this extended command, will be enough to occupy and maintain our
sovereignty over the various rivers from Senegal to
the Gold Coast—a sovereignty which I will procure
from the natives, if approved of, at a small expense; and
I will establish and maintain the British flag on them,
which will cause them to be considered British waters,
and give us the power to exclude all nations from them."

Dated 18th October, 1825.

" On approaching the Sherbro, I caused the king
and chiefs of the maritime districts engaged in the
war, to be assembled; and as they had already applied
to me for protection against their enemies, I informed
them that the only condition upon which I would
grant them effectual security would be the giving up
for ever the Slave Trade, making over to me for the
King of England the sovereignty of their territories,
acknowledging the laws of England, laying down
their arms in the present war, and agreeing never to
undertake any other without the consent of the government of Sierra Leone for the time being. They
immediately agreed to these terms, and a treaty was
accordingly signed and ratified, in presence of all the
people.

* * * *

" By this treaty, upwards of 100 miles of sea-coast

are added to this colony ; a circumstance which, in this particular case, will tend greatly to increase its trade and general prosperity.

*   *   *   *

" As regards the Slave Trade the district now ceded has, for many years back, been the theatre of its most active operations in this or perhaps any other part of the coast ; and the best information that I can collect warrants my stating the number annually exported at not less than 15,000, all of whom will in future be employed in cultivating the soil, preparing and collecting articles of export, and improving their own condition.

*   *   *   *

" The other parties engaged in the war, and who are an inland people, I sent a messenger to, to desire that they would no longer carry on the war, as I had taken the country under my protection ; they expressed the willingness for peace, and some of the principal men among them came down and begged to be *taken under our protection*, which was done.   I could not remain long enough in the Sherbro to receive the more distant ones ; but I make no doubt I shall be able to bring about a general peace throughout these countries, and cause the kings and chiefs to turn their attention to more humane and profitable pursuits.

*   *   *   *

" The affairs of this colony (Sierra Leone) are taking a much wider range, and the valuable pro-

ducts of the interior are finding their way here in much larger proportion than formerly, and the influx of strangers from very distant nations is very great. The name and character of the colony are spreading rapidly, as is proved by the *repeated messengers sent to me from the rulers of distant nations*, and *the eagerness with which they seek our friendship and alliance*. Our influence and authority with the smaller states immediately around are getting greater, and the beneficial results very visible.   *   *   *   *
" The most powerful of them, the king of the Mandingoes, has placed himself under our orders."

Dated 1st November, 1825.

" I have just received from chiefs to the northward of this colony, an offer to give us the sovereignty of their country, and to abolish for ever the Slave Trade, receiving in return, our protection and the benefits of a free trade with us."

Dated 20th December, 1825.

Reports the success of his expedition up the rivers Rokell and Port Logo, which, by their junction, form the river and harbour of Sierra Leone. The Rokell is the direct route to the countries round the source of the Niger.

*   *   *   *

Having overcome the difficulties which had called for his active interference, General Turner entered into a Convention with the people, the substance of which I give in his own words :—

" The Convention, in the first place, puts an effective stop to all slave-trading, to internal wars, a scourge more baneful to Africa than the Slave Trade itself, and gives security and stability to persons and property : it causes the chiefs and others to become industrious, in order to procure, either by cultivation or trade, those articles of luxury which they formerly acquired by the sale of slaves or plunder in war; it will lead to civilization, morality, and a desire of education and useful knowledge, by showing the advantage which educated men will have in trade over uneducated ones; and the becoming provinces of this government will create a strong desire to learn our language and religion.

"To us it will have the effect of greatly extending the sphere of our mercantile transactions, by enabling agents and travellers to pass through the country in security, of extending and improving our geographical knowledge, of obtaining correct information of the power, wealth, and resources of each nation, and thereby forming, in the course of time, a large outlet for our manufactured goods, and of receiving, in return, valuable raw materials, and of spreading throughout distant nations impressions of our wealth, influence, and greatness.   These facts are already beginning to be felt, and the surrounding countries generally, (with the exception of a few factious chiefs who live by plundering travellers,) aware of the advantage of being connected with Sierra Leone, are petitioning this Government to interfere to put an end to their wars, and to take them under its protection.   Your Lordship will observe, *that the public are put to no expense for the accomplishment of these objects ;* that there is no increase of our military establishments required.

*   *   *   *

" I would submit that a small yearly salary should be given to each native chief placed in charge of these provinces or districts, from 50*l.* to 100*l.* per year."

I have given these extracts at considerable length, because they are highly valuable, as showing, on the testimony of a person who had great experience, that the true way to suppress the Slave Trade, and to extricate Africa from its present abyss of misery, is to be found in friendly intercourse with the natives; in the encouragement of their legitimate trade ; in the cultivation of the soil, and in alliances with them for the suppression of the Slave traffic. Acting upon this system, he says, " I have little doubt but I shall have the honour, ere long, to announce to your Lordship the total abolition of the Slave Trade for 1000 miles around me, and a tenfold increase to the trade of this colony."

I may be permitted to relate the melancholy, but to me highly interesting termination of the career of this officer. In the early part of the spring of 1826, he proceeded to the Sherbro country, for the purpose of consolidating those arrangements for the abolition of the Slave Trade which he had entered into with the king and the native chiefs.   On his

arrival at the Sherbro, he discovered, that the great
slave-traders, who had retired from that district on
the signing of the convention, prohibiting the exportation of slaves, had joined with those of the Gallinas,
and had come to the resolution of establishing the
Slave Trade by force, even in the districts where it
had been voluntarily given up by the native chiefs,
and were then assembled in force up the Boom river,
seizing our people, and putting at defiance our power
and our rights.

Upon this band of miscreants he made a successful attack, and he concludes his despatch on the 2nd
of March, 1826, by saying: "After carrying away
the guns and stores, and destroying by fire the town
and neighbourhood, we embarked, and got safely to
the shipping in the Sherbro on the 23rd, after destroying the two principal strongholds, with eight
smaller towns, where these wretches kept their
victims in chains, until the ships were ready to receive
them ; and I sincerely trust that this lesson will teach
the deluded of this country not to put further faith
in the vain boastings of these wicked people, who,
by administering to the worst passions of the ignorant and unfortunate inhabitants, *not only depopu-
late and turn into deserts the most fertile plains
which I have ever seen*, but so blunt their feelings,
and brutalize their natures, that, for a few bottles of
rum and heads of tobacco, the parent is found, without remorse, casting away his offspring ; each village
is engaged against the other, for the purpose of

making prisoners; and men, like beasts of prey, are ever on the watch to seize their neighbours and their fellow-men."

I received an account of this expedition from a gentleman who joined it as a volunteer. He spoke of the conduct of General Turner with admiration. Not content with heading the attack, and commanding the boats in the descent, he took with his own hands the soundings of every part of the river, and underwent more physical toil than the lowest of the crew. He paid the greatest attention to the health of all his party, and administered medicine to them upon the slightest symptom of incipient fever. The only point of which he was regardless was his own health; and to this imprudence he fell a victim. One of his officers ventured to remonstrate with him on the subject, and told him that he saw he was indisposed. The General replied, that nothing could touch his iron constitution; that he never had taken a dose of physic, and never would. On his arrival at Sierra Leone, he wrote with his own hands the despatch dated March 2nd, from which I have already made quotations. On the 3rd of March he begins a short letter to Lord Bathurst thus:—" I lament exceedingly that an attack of fever got up the Boom river should prevent my having the honour of submitting to your Lordship observations upon the bearings which the circumstances detailed in my despatch of the 2nd inst. have upon the state of this unhappy country, and the prospects which they hold out, for a great revolution in the affairs of the inhabitants." After adverting, in three lines to the expedition, he says :—" Although the bar of the Gallinas river is an extremely difficult and hazardous undertaking, I think that, by blockading them, and making a strong party there, I shall completely break up the Slave Trade, and stop for ever, from those shores, the export of near 30,000 slaves annually, substituting agriculture, security of person and property, industry, civilization, and knowledge of the Christian religion. At all events, if my health is restored, I will do my best."

According to my informant, he found the General at his desk, quite insensible, with his pen still in his hand, and this letter before him. It is well worth notice that, in his last words, he should have dwelt upon the extinction of the Slave Trade, by the substitution of agriculture, security of person and property, industry, civilization, and knowledge of the Christian religion.

The effect of General Turner's measures are thus described by his successor, in a despatch, dated 2nd of July, 1826 :—

" The measures adopted by General Turner have secured peace, safety, and tranquillity to a large extent of country, have destroyed an annual export of at least 15,000 slaves, and have prevented all the wretchedness, misery, and bloodshed which would otherwise have attended the making of these slaves.

*   *   *   *

"More real service has been performed by him towards the abolition of the Slave Trade, and that, too, permanently, *should his measures be followed up*, than by all the other means employed by His Majesty's Government for that purpose."

I cannot express how deeply I deplore that twelve years should have elapsed, in which little or no ing has been done by the Government in furtherance of views so sound, so enlightened, and so promising.

Colonel Nicholls, who was Governor of Fernando Po, during our occupation of that island, and who has had, perhaps, as much knowledge, derived from experience, as any man, of the nature of the Slave Trade, and of the most effectual modes of preventing it, in a memorial to Government in 1830, thus describes his general view :—

"There is one means, and I am persuaded but one effectual means, of destroying the Slave Trade, which is, by introducing a liberal and well-regulated system of commerce on the coast of Africa. At present, the African is led to depend principally on the slave-dealers for his supplies of manufactured articles, of which he is so fond, and stands so much in need. The individuals engaged in this traffic are persons of the most infamous and unprincipled description : they come in their ships to the mouths of the different unexplored rivers, where they land a quantity of trade goods of the worst kind, and leaving their supercargoes to exchange them with the chiefs for slaves, return to the sea whilst their cargoes are collecting, where, as pirates, they rob our merchant-ships, murder their crews, and, when glutted with plunder, return to the coast to ship their victims, for whom they pay about 7*l.* or 8*l.* a-piece, and sell them for 70*l.*, 80*l.*, or 100*l.* each. In conducting the barter for these poor creatures with the chiefs, the slavers are frequently guilty of every sort of violence and injustice. Of this the chiefs are well aware, and submit to it only because they have no redress. Were it put in their power to procure better manufactured goods from merchants who would have some regard to justice and fair dealing in their transactions with them, they would eagerly give them the preference, particularly if they were protected from the resentment of the slave-dealers.

" I will give, as nearly as I can recollect, the substance of a conversation which passed between one of the native chiefs and myself on this subject. I began by asking him how he could act so unwisely as to sell his countrymen for 7*l.* or 8*l.*, when he might render them so much more profitable to him, by making them labour? The chief mused awhile, and then said, ' If you will show me how this is to be done, I will take your advice.' I asked him how much palm-oil a man could collect during the season? ' From one to two tuns,' was his answer. I then inquired, how a man could be employed when it was not the palm-oil season? ' In cutting down and squaring wood, gathering elephants' teeth, tending

K

cattle, and cultivating rice, corn, and yams,' was the reply. I then said to him, ' Suppose a man collects a tun and a half of palm-oil in a season; that, according to its present value, will amount to 11*l.* or 12*l.*; and suppose he picks up one elephant's tooth, the value of which is about 2*s.* per lb., the weight frequently fifty pounds; but reckon it at one-half that weight, that will be 2*l.* 10*s.* more. The value of these two articles alone will be nearly double what his price brings you, if you sell him; and this he would bring you every year, allowing him all the other kinds of his labour for his own maintenance. Upon this simple calculation, the truth of which cannot be denied, what a loser you are by selling him. Besides, you get goods inferior, both in quality and quantity, to those you could procure by exchanging the produce of this man's labour with British merchants.' The chief acknowledged I was right; but said that, when I was gone, the slavers would come, and if he did not get slaves for them, they would burn his town, and perhaps take away himself and his family, in place of the slaves they expected him to collect for them; but that if this could be prevented, he would sell no more slaves. I then told him, if he promised this, I would come to his assistance, in case the slavers committed any violence against him, and put the miscreants in his power: that I should advise him to assemble his head-men, and try and punish the delinquents by his own law, and I thought they would not trouble him again. I assured him, that he and his countrymen were considered by us as much better men than these slavers, and that we would protect them if they would trade fairly with us in other produce than slaves.

" This chief drove off the first slaver that came, as I directed him : he is now carrying on a thriving trade, and his people are more civil and kind to us than any I have yet seen. I feel convinced that I could influence all the chiefs along the coast in the same manner ; but, to be able to effect this, it would be necessary to have the means of moving from one place to another, with a degree of celerity that a steam-vessel alone could give us. This would be requisite, both to enable us to keep our promise of protecting the chiefs from the slavers, and also for the purpose of going up the rivers, which are at present unknown to us, with the least possible risk of health, or loss of time.

" Steam-boats would also be of incalculable use to commerce, by towing ships over bars and agitated currents, whilst, as a means of catching the slave-ships, and protecting the coast from the depredations of their crews, three steamers would effect more than the expensive squadron now maintained there. These three vessels should carry four heavy guns each, be of as light a draught of water as possible, and be manned with fifty white * and fifty black men each : they would not cost one-half as much as one large frigate, one corvette, and two gun-brigs, whilst they

* Colonel Nicholls now thinks that a much smaller number of white sailors would be sufficient.

K 2

would be an infinitely more efficient means of attaining the end proposed by the use of them. I pledge myself to put an end to the whole of our expense, and totally to suppress the Slave Trade in two years. But if this plan be not adopted, we may go on paying over and over again for the liberated Africans to the end of time, without performing anything beneficial in their behalf."

Mr. Rendall, who was Governor of the Gambia, (where he died,) it appears, contemplated, some years ago, a plan for the suppression of the Slave Trade ; and had made some progress in a letter intended to be addressed to the Duke of Wellington. I extract a few passages from it, which will serve to show, that experience conducted him to the same conclusion as that which has been arrived at by the authorities I have already cited. In the introduction, he says—" Of all the measures calculated to insure the prosperity of Africa, none promises so well as the encouragement of its legitimate commerce and agriculture." He recommends the immediate clearance and cultivation of a district, " which would at once embrace two of the most important objects ; viz., the improvement in salubrity, and the production of such articles of export as would render the colony valuable to the mother country." " Give," he says, " an impulse to industry by establishing model plantations ; let moral and religious education go hand in hand; and thus most firmly do I believe that the great and benevolent objects of the real friends of

Africa will be most securely attained."—" Government," he adds, " must begin, by showing to the natives the practicability and profit of cultivation." But he is convinced that the outlay thus required would be speedily and abundantly repaid. He speaks of cotton, coffee, indigo, and ginger as being the produce that would thrive the best.

I now insert some extracts, bearing on the same points, which I find in Mr. M'Queen's " View of Northern Central Africa :"—

" There is no efficient way to arrest the progress of this deep-rooted evil, but to teach the negroes useful knowledge, and the arts of civilized life. Left to themselves, the negroes will never effectually accomplish this. It must be done by a mighty power, who will take them under its protection,—a power sufficiently bold, enlightened, and just, to burst asunder the chains of that grovelling superstition which enthrals and debases their minds, and that, with the voice of authority, can unite the present jarring elements which exist in Africa, and direct them to honourable and useful pursuits. Till the native princes are taught that they may be rich without selling men,—and till Africa is shown that it is in the labour and industry of her population, and in the cultivation of her soil, that true wealth consists,— and till that population see a power, which can protect them from such degrading bondage, there can be no security for liberty or property in Africa;

and, consequently, no wish or hope for improvement amongst her population.

* * * *

" It is in Africa that this evil must be rooted out,— by African hands and African exertions chiefly that it can be destroyed. It is a waste of time and a waste of means, an aggravation of the disorder, to keep lopping off the smaller branches of a malignant, a vigorous, and reproductive plant, while the root and stem remain uninjured, carefully supplied with nourishment, and beyond our reach. Half the sums we have expended in this manner would have rooted up slavery for ever. Only teach them, and show them that we will give them more for their produce than for the hand that rears it, and the work is done. All other methods and means will prove ineffectual.

* * * *

" The change contemplated in Africa could not be wrought in a day. But were we once firmly established, in a commanding attitude on the Niger, and an end put to the two great scourges of Africa, Superstition and an external Slave Trade, the progress of improvement would be rapid, and the advantages great.

* * * *

" Nothing can be done,—nothing ever will be done, to alter their present indolent and inactive mode of life, till justice and general security are spread throughout these extensive regions. It would be

vain to expect industry or exertion on their parts, in
order to procure the comforts and the luxuries of life,
when no one can call anything he may possess his
own, or where the superior wealth which he does
possess serves only to mark him out as the prey of
the unfeeling robber or sovereign despot."

The opinions also of travellers, who have visited
different parts of Africa at different times, are very
similar, both as to the capabilities of Africa, and as to
the opposite effects produced by the antagonist systems of the Slave Trade and legitimate commerce;
and they concur in declaring that the encouragement of the one ever tends to the destruction of the
other. This truth was admitted even by Golberry,
who was so far from being carried away by the phan-
toms of philanthropy,—that he owns he felt some
difficulty in checking the expression of his " just
indignation" against the " cruel theories" of those
pretended philosophers, who imposed on the vulgar
by decrying the Slave Trade.

" I have also observed," says Golberry, " that this
surface of Africa (all the country between Cape
Blanco and Cape Palmas), is at least 374,400 square
leagues, which is more than a fifth of the total
superficies of this large continent; and that, if we
should one day be enabled to traverse freely and habitually this extensive space, not only Europe would
discover new sources of wealth, and new objects for
industry, but that, by a natural and inevitable consequence, the whole of Africa would soon be enlight-

ened, and everything which yet remains ambiguous in the centre of this continent would be laid open to investigation.

"There is reason to presume that more active relations, together with agricultural and mercantile establishments, and wholesome institutions, whose object should be the instruction and civilization of the negroes, would, in the course of fifteen years, augment these products from thirty to more than sixty millions ;* and if, during this period, England and France act in unison—if the Governments of the two first nations in the world were to proceed, with emulation, in pursuit of the same object, then, far from the Slave Trade being augmented, it would soon diminish to one half, and it would quickly be abolished by a natural consequence ; the inexhaustible fertility of a soil which the natives would learn to cultivate, and which has hitherto remained, in a manner of speaking, abandoned to nature, would administer to the wants and enjoyments of Europe ; the African would become civilized ; and the ardent wishes of a rational philosophy would speedily be accomplished."

Robertson speaks to the same effect :—"If Africa is to be made subservient to the views of Europe, let her have an interest in her own labour, and that interest will be the strongest and best security for her friendship. Show her the advantages

* Francs.

of industry, and will she deviate so far from the
usual motives which actuate mankind, as not to cultivate such a connexion, in order to improve her
own condition? There is but one system for us,
which can secure her friendship, and her social intercourse, and that is, an equitable use of our and
her rights."

Park's testimony is similar :—" It cannot, however, admit of a doubt that all the rich and valuable productions, both of the East and West
Indies might easily be naturalized, and brought
to the utmost perfection, in the tropical parts of
this immense continent. Nothing is wanting to
this end but example, to enlighten the minds of
the natives ; and instruction, to enable them to direct their industry to proper objects. It was not
possible for me to behold the wonderful fertility of
the soil, the vast herds of cattle, proper both for
labour and food, and a variety of other circumstances favourable to colonization and agriculture,
and reflect, withal, on the means which presented
themselves of a vast inland navigation, without lamenting that a country, so abundantly gifted and
favoured by nature, should remain in its present
savage and neglected state. Much more did I lament
that a people, of manners and disposition so gentle
and benevolent, should either be left, as they now are,
immersed in the gross and uncomfortable blindness
of pagan superstition, or permitted to become converts to a system of bigotry and fanaticism which,

without enlightening the mind, often debases the heart."

Mr. Laird, discussing the best mode of establishing trade, and of civilizing Africa, proposes establishing a chain of British posts up the Niger, and across to the Gambia : he proposes six or seven stations, and says :—"There are two ways in which this might be done with comparative economy : the one, by merely establishing a trading post; the other, by acquiring a small territory and importing West Indian and American free negroes, who would bring with them the knowledge they have acquired in the cultivation of sugar and other tropical produce, and would form, in fact, agricultural schools for the benefit of the surrounding population."

" By the Niger, the whole of Western Africa would be embraced ; by the Sharry (which I have no doubt will be found navigable to the meridian of 25° east longitude) a communication would be opened with all the nations inhabiting the unknown countries between the Niger and the Nile. British influence and enterprise would thereby penetrate into the remotest recesses of the country; one hundred millions of people would be brought into direct contact with the civilized world ; new and boundless markets would be opened to our manufactures; a continent teeming with inexhaustible fertility would yield her riches to our traders; not merely a nation, but hundreds of nations, would be awakened from the lethargy of centuries, and become useful and active

members of the great commonwealth of mankind :
and every British station would become a centre from
whence religion and commerce would radiate their
influence over the surrounding country. Who can
calculate the effect that would be produced, if such
a plan were followed out, and Africa, freed from her
chains, moral and physical, allowed to develope her
energies in peace and security? No parallel can be
drawn, no comparison can be instituted, between
Africa enslaved, and Africa free and unfettered."

Lander confirms these views :—" It is more than
probable, as we have now ascertained, that a water
communication may be carried on with so extensive
a part of the interior of Africa, that a considerable trade will be opened with the country through
which we have passed. The natives only require
to know what is wanted from them, and to be shown
what they will have in return, and much produce
that is now lost, from neglect, will be turned to a
considerable account. The countries situated on
the banks of the Niger will become frequented
from all the adjacent parts, and this magnificent
stream will assume an appearance it has never yet
displayed."

Major Gray, summing up the means for bringing
the Africans to a state of civilization, and relieving
the people from the tyranny of their chiefs, says,—
" It has occurred to me there are no means more
available, and, I may add, more speedily practicable,

than the enlargement of our intercourse with the
people, and the encouragement and protection of the
internal commerce of Africa. By this, we can improve them in the way of example; by the other, we
can benefit them and ourselves in the way of inter-
change of commodity: our habits and our manners
will gain upon them in time, and our skill tend to
stimulate and encourage theirs."

" By increasing their commerce, we also obtain
another happy consummation, we give them employment, and we consequently, to a certain extent, secure
them from the incessant meddling of their maraboos.
We could congregate them in greater numbers together, and therefore the more readily instruct them;
and I may venture to add, that if a fair trial of zeal
were used in such a delightful employment, within
a very few years they would prove themselves not
unfitted for the enjoyment of liberal institutions."

" That there are powers of mind in the African,
it were quite idle to dispute; that the productions of
the country are capable of being beneficially employed must, I think, be equally incontestable to any
one who has carefully perused the preceding pages;
and, to act with honesty, we should not allow both, or
either, to lie for ever dormant."

" The European governments," says Burckhardt
" who have settlements on the coasts of Africa, may
contribute to it by commerce, and by the introduction
among the negroes of arts and industry."

Capt. W. Allen, R.N.,* in a letter addressed to me August, 1839, observes:—"I have read your 'Remedy' with great interest and attention, the more so, as I find embodied in it all the ideas I had formed on the same subject, deduced from observations written on the spot."

There is no species of argument which carries with it a greater force of conviction to my mind, than the concurrence of a variety of persons, who, being competent to judge, and having opportunities of forming a sound judgment, examine a given object with very different purposes, from very different points of view, yet arrive, without concert, or previous communication, at the same conclusion. In the case before us, we collect the unpublished despatches, letters, and journals of the several Governors of Sierra Leone, Fernando Po, the Gambia, and the Gold Coast. These documents were written at different times, with no view to publication, and there was no connection between the officers who wrote them. Differing on many points, they harmonise exactly on those which affect my case. Each speaks of the exuberant fertility of the soil; each laments the desolation which, in spite of nature, prevails; and each looks to the cultivation of those fertile lands, and to the growth of legitimate commerce, as the remedy to the distractions of Africa, and the horrors of the Slave Trade. For example, it appears that General Turner at

* Captain W. Allen was employed by the Admiralty to ascend the Niger in Laird and Oldfield's expedition.

Sierra Leone, and Colonel Nicolls of Fernando Po,
had in view much such a plan as I have suggested,
when they spoke in their despatches of putting an
end to the Slave Trade in two or three years.   This
unconscious union between themselves is not all.
The views of these gentlemen correspond with those
which I find in the private journals of the Mission-.
aries, who have gathered their experience, and formed
their opinion, while labouring among the native tribes
of the Gambia.   That which is the opinion of these
soldiers and of these teachers of religion turns out to
be the opinion of the most distinguished travellers
and of intelligent traders.   Captain Becroft, who
traded on the Western Coast, and Captain Raymond,
who did the same on the Eastern, tell me,—that
trade, springing from the cultivation of the soil, will,
and that nothing else will, abolish the Slave Trade.

This uniformity of opinion between governors and
missionaries, travellers and traders, stops not here.
Mr. M'Queen and Mr. Clarkson,* who have spent
their lives in studying Africa, but not in the same
school, here cease to differ.   Mr. Clarkson thus concludes a long letter to me, dated November 20th,
1838 (after having noticed and approved each suggestion I had made, particularly the purchase of a
large tract of country, for the establishment of pattern
farms, and the selection of Fernando Po) : —
" Upon the whole, it is my opinion that, if Govern-

* For Mr. Clarkson's judgment on the views and principles
stated in this book, see Appendix D.

ment would make the settlements which you have
pointed out; if they were to substitute steamers in the
place of sailing ships; if they were, by annual presents,
to work upon the native chiefs; if they were to buy
the land upon which their settlements would be built,
and introduce pattern farms for the cultivation of cotton, indigo, rice, or whatever other tropical production
they might think fit, they might as certainly count upon
the abolition of the Slave Trade, even in a short time,
as upon any unknown event, which men might expect
to be produced, from right reasoning, or by going the
right way to work, in order to produce it. As far as
our knowledge of Africa, and African manners, customs, and dispositions goes, a better plan could not be
devised—no other plan, in short, could answer. Had
this plan been followed from the first, it would have
done wonders for Africa by this time, and it would
do much for us now : in two years from the trial of it
it would become doubtful, whether it was worth while
to carry on the Slave Trade ; and in five years I have
no doubt that it would be generally, though, perhaps,
not totally, abandoned. Depend upon it, there is no
way of civilizing and christianizing Africa, which all
good men must look to, but this." " Teach them,"
says Mr. M'Queen, " that we will give them more
for their produce, than for the hand that rears it, and
the work is done. All other methods and means
will prove ineffectual."

Other illustrations of this coincidence might be
quoted. The Society of Friends, anxious to benefit

Africa, could devise no better means, than the establishment of a school and a farm in the neighbourhood
of St. Mary's.   The experiment failed, or it seemed
to fail, owing to the death of the agent whom they
had sent; but it was with no small pleasure that I
found, in the papers of the brother of a deceased
governor of the colony, this evidence that their
labours were not entirely lost.   After stating that the
Society had formerly established a school and a farm
on a point of land forming Cape St. Mary's, " as
eligible a spot for such an undertaking as could be
found in the country," he goes on to say, "The natives
of the neighbourhood must have observed, with some
degree of attention, the mode adopted by these settlers
in their agricultural pursuits.   Indeed, it must be
inferred that many of them assisted on the works of
the farm, as at this date (viz. 14 years after) they
conduct matters in a more neat and satisfactory manner than is to be observed in other parts of the
country.   Their grounds are well cleaned and enclosed ; vegetation, of one kind or another, appears
to be kept up during the year ; the quality of their
articles is superior to their neighbours; and altogether there is a superiority among these people, a
neatness about their persons and villages, that pleases
the eye, particularly as these things do not exist in
other parts of the country.   The old chief of the
district loses no opportunity of making the most particular inquiries after his friends the Quakers, and
of expressing his regret that such good people should

not have remained amongst them, as their kindness will ever live in the memory of the inhabitants. The chief and his sons are worthy good folks, and much attached to the English. The seeds which Mr. W. Allen and other gentlemen have sent to the Gambia have been of infinite service, in improving the quality of the cotton and rice."*

I hardly know anything more encouraging than the facts which have thus unexpectedly come to light. Here an effort has been made, exactly in conformity with the views which I am endeavouring to urge, but it was soon abandoned; yet the effect of that imperfect experiment is still visible in the improvement of the face of the country, and in the manifest distinction between that district which had been thus befriended, and the desolate regions which surround it.

The fact, too, that these simple people retain a lively and grateful recollection of their benefactors, and cease not to pant for their return, proves that in the minds of the people, as well as in the quality of the soil, there are materials on which we may work. When so much was effected by a slight effort, what may we not expect to be accomplished, when the same merciful measures shall be adopted permanently, and upon a large scale?

One further coincidence, and not the least remarkable, remains to be stated. I gave a description on a former occasion† of a slave-hunt, or gazzua,

* Rendall. † Page 91 of this edition.

L

which was perpetrated in the dominions, and by
the permission of the Pasha of Egypt. Some
strong representations of the impolicy and atrocity
of such proceedings were made to him by some of
our countrymen, particularly by Dr. Bowring.* And
I have now to describe the influence which these have
exercised over his conduct.† From a manuscript
which purports to be an official account of the journey of his Highness to Soudan, of the views in which
it originated, and of the policy which was adopted
with regard to the natives, I extract the following
particulars. In the autumn of 1838 the Pasha's
attention was turned to his savage territory of Soudan, and he resolved to take measures for the abolition
of the Slave Trade, and to introduce a reformation in
the customs, commerce, and agriculture of the inhabitants: for this purpose he repaired thither in
person, accompanied by his usual attendants, and
several scientific persons, collected not only from his
own country, but from the continent of Europe. He
embarked in a steam-boat, October 15th, 1838. In
passing the cataracts, he had to endure some hard-

---

* Vide Appendix E., p. 564, for an extract from a letter from
Sir. W. H. Pearson to Mr. Buxton, junior, containing an account
of that gentleman's visit on board a slave-ship on the Nile.

† The consul at Alexandria, of date 5th May, 1838, narrates a
conversation which he had had with Mahommed Ali, in which the
pasha said that he would not permit his officers in the interior to
seize slaves: and he adds that the pasha himself does not now
purchase any more slaves for his own use or service.—Class D.,
1838-9, p. 14.

ships, and was exposed to considerable danger.
After passing the first cataract, he had to remain
during a night without provisions or attendance : in
the attempt to pass the second, the boat in which he
was seated was dashed violently on the rocks, and it
was with difficulty that he effected his escape, while
the vessel was carried away by the current. On the
eleventh of November, the cataract of Annek was
reached : it appears from the narrative, that this was
the first attempt that was ever made to pass it : from
Dongola, he went across the desert to Kartoum, the
capital of Sennaar, on the confluence of the Blue and
the White Nile; he proceeded along the Blue Nile,
and there was joined by some pupils of the schools
of language and mineralogy. At Fazoglo, hearing
of depredations, committed, according to custom, by
a tribe of mountaineers on their more feeble neighbours, he despatched a force against them, under the
command of a superior officer, who returned with
540 prisoners. His Highness had them brought
before him, and spoke to them at great length on
the odiousness and barbarity of stealing and selling
their fellow-creatures ; then, wishing to join example
to precept, he permitted them to depart, after having
distributed to every one ten days' provisions and
given dresses to five of the chiefs. Learning that
some prisoners had been taken at Kordofan, he
ordered them to be dismissed, with permission to
return home, or to establish themselves as cultivators
on the banks of the White Nile, issuing at the same

time a manifesto, declaring that slave-hunting was strictly forbidden ; and that if any quarrels should arise between neighbouring tribes, their differences were to be brought before the Governor-general, who was commissioned to decide them. At length he arrived at the mouth of Fazangoro, where, after inspecting the gold mines, he laid the foundations of a town, which is to be called by his own name, Mohammed Ali, and to contain houses for fifteen hundred families. The chiefs of the country showed their readiness to co-operate with him, by offering a much larger force for the working of the mines : this however he declined. We are expressly told, that he pays his workmen wages, and provides them with dresses adapted to the climate : also, that he granted land to Arab agriculturists for the formation of model farms, supplied them with the necessary implements and animals, and declared them to be exempt from taxes for five years. The land of Sennaar is extremely fertile ; it readily returns sixty for one ; the dourah grows quickly and produces very rich ears ; animals and wood abound ; cotton succeeds wonderfully, almost without cost, and it produces more wool than that of Egypt, which is cultivated at a great expense. Hitherto, however, cultivation has been entirely neglected. The Pasha collected round him a great number of the sheikhs, made them presents, and addressed them in a speech, remarkable not only for its good sense, but for the quarter from whence it was delivered. " The people of other parts of the

world were formerly savages; they have had instructors, and, by labour and perseverance, they have
civilized themselves; you have heads and hands like
them ; do as they have done : you also will raise yourselves to the rank of men ; you will acquire great
riches, and will taste enjoyments of which you can at
present, from your profound ignorance, form no conception.   Nothing is wanting for this purpose : you
have a great quantity of land, cattle, and wood : your
population is numerous, the men strong, and the women fruitful.   Up to the present time you have had no
guide : you have one now :—it is I !—I will lead you
to civilization and happiness.   The world is divided
into five great parts ; that which you occupy is called
Africa : in every country, except this, the value of
labour is understood, and a taste for good and useful
things prevails ; men devote themselves with ardour to
commerce, which produces wealth, pleasure, and glory
—words, which you cannot even comprehend.   Egypt
itself is not an extensive country ; yet, thanks to labour and the industry of its inhabitants, it is rich,
and will become more so : distant provinces are acquainted with it ; and the territory of Sennaar, which
is twenty times larger than Egypt, produces almost
nothing, because its inhabitants remain as idle as if
they were without life.   Understand well that labour produces all things ; and that without labour
nothing can be had."

His Highness then explained to them, in detail,
the advantages of agriculture and commerce. His

auditors, astonished at what they heard, begged him
earnestly to take them into Egypt, that they might
be instructed in those arts. " It would be better,"
replied his Highness, " that you should send your
children there ; they will learn more easily, because
they are younger, and will remain longer useful
to these countries, when they return to them. I
will place them in my colleges ; they will learn
there all that is useful and ornamental. Be not
uneasy about their welfare, they shall be my adopted
children ; and, when they are sufficiently instructed in
the sciences, I will send them back to be happiness
to you, and to these countries, and a glory to you."

The sheikhs very willingly accepted the offer :—
every one wished to send his children into Egypt ;
the most powerful among them, named Abd-el-Ka-
dir, having no son, asked the favour for his nephew.
His Highness then urgently recommended Ahmed
Pasha to labour for the welfare and civilization of
these people ; and, for the purpose of encouragement,
announced, that he should himself return next year,
in order to judge the progress that might be made,
and incite them to fresh exertions.

The Viceroy departed the next morning, and returned to Fazoglo on the 1st of February, when he
renewed his exhortations to the sheikhs of that dis
trict ; and proceeded to Kartoum, where he was delighted to find the good effects of his late visit, in
some land being already in full cultivation. From
thence he visited, in like manner, the White Nile,

and, on returning to Kartoum, he set on foot the building of a Christian church. Before leaving the place, he proclaimed the freedom of trade in indigo, which the provinces of Dongola and Berber produce in considerable quantities, and ordered the governor to supply implements, and everything necessary, for the development of its cultivation. After which, he embarked with his suite, leaving M. Lambert, with the charge of making two reports,—the one, upon a projected railroad, in that part of the desert which separates Abu-Muhammed from Kurusku; the other, on the formation of a canal between the White River and Kordofan, destined to furnish water for the irrigation of the land, and to facilitate the carriage of the iron-ore of the mines.

The cataracts were repassed on his return; and, on the 14th of March, the cannon of the citadel of Cairo announced to Egypt the arrival of the Viceroy, after an absence of five months and four days.

Having freely, in another place, commented upon the conduct of the Pasha, in permitting the continuance of the gazzua, and in allowing his officers to reimburse themselves, for any arrears of their pay, with the human booty which they might seize, we are bound to do justice to the course which he has now pursued, and to acknowledge that the zeal and energy which he has displayed, in acting upon his new opinions, furnish an example, which any civilized and Christian nation may do itself honour by following. It must be confessed, there were great

impediments in his way : it was not likely that he, a
follower of Mahomet, whose religion justifies the enslavement of the infidel, should have shared our abhorrence of all that pertains to the trade in man : he
must have had to surmount many strong and deep-
seated prejudices in his own bosom, and must have
exposed himself to public reproach, if not danger,
before he resolved to set his face against a system so
long established, and so lucrative. It was an act
of great vigour in a prince, seventy years of age,
threatened by a formidable enemy, and holding his
authority in some considerable measure, by his own
personal presence and influence, to undertake a journey, of more than five months' duration, through a
country so rarely visited, exposing himself to considerable perils and fatigue, and the expense of conveying with him a large body of well-qualified
assistants. It is greatly to the credit of his understanding to have seen so distinctly that a greater
amount of wealth may be drawn from the cultivation
of the soil, than from the chase and capture of the
inhabitants. The language which he uses to the
native chiefs proves that he well comprehends the
principles by which a degree of civilization may be
spread among savage tribes, and valuable products
reared from their rich but untilled lands. But the
point which deserves most notice is, that, from the
moment he was convinced, he acted, at once and
boldly. In a very short period, he has executed a
voyage of discovery ; he has selected an excellent posi-

tion for a town, and commenced building it. He has
entered upon a system of hiring labour and paying
wages (in itself, I am afraid, an innovation) ; he has
laboured to convince the native chiefs that it is better
to sell their productions than their subjects : he
has made some provision for the education of their
children ; he has relinquished taxes, and established
free trade in articles which have hitherto been subject to a monopoly ; he has given orders for the formation of a canal and a railroad ; and he is employed in
opening through the cataracts a way sufficiently wide
for the passage of boats of large dimensions : moreover, and it confirms one of my most important anti-
cipations, he has found better cotton in Soudan than
that which is grown by himself in Egypt : in short, if
I may judge by his actions, as represented in the narrative which is put forth under his authority, there is
no more thorough-going advocate of the policy which
I am labouring to recommend to the British nation
than the personage whom, but a few months ago, I
had to point out to public indignation as the patron
of the horrible gazzua. It must, however, be borne
in memory that we have only seen the BEGINNING of
a new system. The character of the Pasha will be
judged, not by what he has hitherto attempted, but by
the fidelity with which he shall adhere to the principles he has professed, and by the sagacity with which
he shall carry into execution the wise and benevolent
design which seems to reflect so much credit upon him.

I have thus shown that many persons, whose

veracity we have no reason to doubt, whose experience furnishes the best means of forming a correct judgment, and who cannot be suspected of acting in concert, arrive at precisely the same conclusions. The argument deducible from this coincidence of opinion enforced itself on me with peculiar effect. I possessed neither the practical experience which belongs to a traveller, a trader, or the governor of a colony, nor the intimate acquaintance with native mind acquired by the missionary; nor that deep knowledge of all that has been written concerning Africa, in which Mr. Clarkson and Mr. M'Queen excel. Yet in ignorance of almost all the opinions to which I have now referred, I had, by a process, and from documents, quite distinct, arrived at the same result. I attentively examined the papers on the Slave Trade, annually presented to Parliament: they demonstrated the unwavering sincerity of the Government, by whatever party administered, and the generous compassion of the nation: at the same time, they forced upon me an undoubting conviction, that the evil could never be eradicated by this mode of correction. Ready to abandon all further effort, in despair of being able to effect any practical good, and from an abhorrence of the task of afflicting myself and others by a recital of evils, which I could not cure, and of horrors, which every effort seemed to aggravate, I cast my eyes, in every direction, in order to discover if there yet existed any effectual remedy. It then occurred to me, that Africa, after all, obtains a very inconsiderable revenue from the Slave Trade; while the outlay, so to speak,—the desolation, the slaughter, the bloody and diabolical superstition, and the human suffering from all these,—are indeed prodigious : the net profit to Africa (whatever it may be to the civilized ruffians who instigate the trade) is miserably scanty. " Thou sellest thy people for nought; and dost not increase thy wealth by their price." There was something hopeful in the fact that the interests of Africa were not involved in the continuance of the Slave Trade. It gave birth to the inquiry, Is it not possible for us to undersell the slave-dealer, and to drive him out of the market, by offering more for the productions of the soil than he ever gave for the bodies of the inhabitants?

This opened a new field of investigation. I eagerly turned to every book of travels which might furnish an insight into the capabilities of that quarter of the globe. There was anything but a dearth of materials : I found evidence, sufficient to fill volumes, that Africa, though now a wilderness, may rank with any portion of the world in natural resources and in the power of production. Travellers, whatever may be the scarcity of other topics, never fail to speak of the exuberance of the soil on the one hand, and the misery of its inhabitants on the other. These two subjects occupy three-fourths of the pages of those who have visited Africa. It is sufficient here to say that I rose from that part of the investigation, in possession of incontrovertible proof that nature had

provided an abundance of all things which consti-
tute agricultural wealth. The question then arises,
Are there hands to till the earth? Africa, notwithstanding the annual and terrible drain of its inhabitants, teems with population : but for the Slave Trade,
there is no reason to doubt that it would be as
densely peopled as any part of the globe. Can
labour be obtained there as cheaply as in Brazil,
Cuba, or the Carolinas? We have some light on
this subject. We know that a slave fetches, in
Interior Africa, about 3*l.* ; in Brazil, at least 70*l.* ;
when seasoned, as an African is in his own country,
100*l.* Africa, then, has this great advantage over America, that it can be cultivated at one-twentieth of the
expense. Why, then, should the inhabitants be torn
from Africa, when her native labourers upon her
native land might hold successful competition with
any Slave State? The soil being equal, a labourer
in Africa will raise as much produce as the same
labourer transported to America, but at less expense ; for you can hire ten labourers in the former
at the price that one costs in the latter. Hence I,
infer, that the labour and produce of Africa, if fairly
called forth, would rival the labour employed, and
the produce raised in America, throughout the
markets of the civilized world.

Besides all this, the labourers stolen in Africa are
not, in fact, carried to America. What the one
loses, the other does not gain. Africa loses three
labourers ; America obtains but one : in no species

of merchandise is there such waste of the *raw* material, as in the merchandise of man.   In what other trade do two-thirds of the goods perish, in order that one-third may reach the market ?

Apart, then, from all considerations of humanity and Christian principle, and narrowing the question to a mere calculation of pecuniary profit, it would appear a strange kind of economy to carry away the population from their native fields, which need nothing but those hands for their cultivation, in order to plant them in diminished numbers, at a prodigious expense, in another hemisphere, and on land not more productive.

But would these men be willing to work for wages ? I did not require to be taught that men will work, not only as well but ten times better, for reward, than they were ever made to do by the lash : proof, however, of this truth presented itself.   As I shall have to enlarge upon that subject before I close this book, I will only say here, that of all the fictions ever invented by interested parties to quiet their own consciences, or delude the world, there is none so gross as the doctrine, that less labour is to be won by wages, than can be extorted by the whip.

Thus, then, the study of the writings of travellers proved to me that Africa possessed all the separate elements necessary for vast production and extensive commerce ; but these materials, were, if I may so express myself, asunder : the hands, both able and willing to labour, had never been brought to bear upon

the land, so capable of yielding a grateful return.
It was not till after I had come to the conclusion
that all that was wanting for the deliverance of
Africa was that agriculture, commerce, and instruction should have a *fair trial*, that I discovered that
those views were not confined to myself, and that
others had arrived, by practical experience, at the
same result which I had learnt from the facts, and
from reasoning upon them; and I was very well
pleased to renounce any little credit which might
attach to the discovery, in exchange for the solid
encouragement and satisfaction of finding that what
was with me but theory, was with them the fruit
of experience.   I cannot but remember that a poet,
who possessed the faculty of combining the closest
reasoning with the most flowing verse, saw, and
availed himself of this species of argument for the
defence of Christianity :—

> " Whence, but from Heaven, could men unskill'd in arts,
>   In several ages born, of several parts,
>   Weave such agreeing truths ; or how, or why,
>   Should all conspire to cheat us with a lie ?"

159

CHAPTER V.

PRINCIPLES.

"True faith, true policy, united run."—POPE.

" If you plant where savages be, do not only entertain them with trifles and gingles, but use them *justly* and *graciously*, with sufficient guard nevertheless."—LORD BACON.

" The greatest advantage a Government can possess is to be the one trustworthy Government in the midst of Governments which nobody can trust.'' —EDINBURGH REVIEW, Jan. 1840.—*Life of Clive*, p. 330.

IT appears to me a matter of such peculiar moment that we should distinctly settle and declare the PRINCIPLES on which our whole intercourse with Africa, whether economic or benevolent, whether directed exclusively to her benefit, or mingled (as I think it may most fairly be) with a view to our own, shall be founded, and by which it shall be regulated, that I venture, though at the risk of being tedious, to devote a separate chapter to the consideration of them. The principles, then, which I trust to see adopted by our country, are these,—

Free Trade.

Free Labour.

FREE TRADE.

Nothing, I apprehend, could be more unfortunate to the continent we wish to befriend, or more discreditable to ourselves, than that Great Britain should give any colour to the suspicion of being actuated by mercenary motives; an apology would thus be afforded to every other nation for any attempt it might make to thwart our purpose. We know, from the Duke of Wellington's despatches, that the powers on the continent were absolutely incredulous as to the purity of the motives which prompted us, at the congress of Aix la Chapelle, to urge, *beyond everything else*, the extinction of the Slave Trade.

In a letter to Mr. Wilberforce, dated Paris, 15th Sept., 1814, the Duke of Wellington says, " It is not believed that we are in earnest about it, or have abolished the trade on the score of its inhumanity. It is thought to have been a commercial speculation ; and that, having abolished the trade ourselves, with a view to prevent the undue increase of colonial produce in our stores, of which we could not dispose, we now want to prevent other nations from cultivating their colonies to the utmost of their power."

And again, in another letter to the Right Honourable J. C. Villiers :—

Paris, 31*st August*, 1814.

" The efforts of Great Britain to put an end to it (the Slave Trade) are not attributed to good motives, but to commercial jealousy, and a desire to keep the monopoly of colonial produce in our own hands."

The grant of twenty millions may have done something to quench these narrow jealousies, but still, the nations of the continent will be slow to believe that we are entirely disinterested. It should, then, be made manifest to the world, by some signal act, that the moving spring is humanity ; that if England makes settlements on the African coast, it is only for the more effectual attainment of her great object ; and that she is not allured by the hopes either of gain or conquest, or by the advantages, national or individual, political or commercial, which may, and I doubt not, will follow the undertaking. Such a demonstration would be given, if, with the declaration, that it is resolved to abolish the Slave Trade, and, that in this cause we are ready, if requisite, to exert all our powers, Great Britain, should couple an official pledge that she will not claim for herself a single benefit, which shall not be shared by every nation uniting with her in the extinction of the Slave Trade ; and especially

First,—That no exclusive privilege in favour of British subjects shall ever be allowed to exist.

Secondly,—That no *custom-house* shall ever be established at Fernando Po.

Thirdly,—That no distinction shall be made there, *whether in peace or in war,* between our own subjects and those of any such foreign power, as to the rights they shall possess, or the terms on which they shall enjoy them. In short, that we purchase Fernando Po, and will hold it for no other purpose than the benefit of Africa. I am well aware that these may appear startling propositions ; I am, how-

M

ever, supported in them by high authorities : the suggestion as to the custom-house was made to me by
Mr. Porter, of the Board of Trade ; and that respecting neutrality in peace or in war, originated with the
learned Judge of the British Vice-Admiralty Courts.
Supported by his authority, I may venture to say
that, thu gh a novel, it would be a noble characteristic
of our colony. As it is intended for different ends, so
it would be ruled by different principles, from any
colony which has ever been undertaken : it would
have the distinction of being the neutral ground of the
world, elevated above the mutual injuries of war ;
where, for the prosecution of a good and a vast object,
the subjects and the fleets of all nations may meet
in amity, and where there shall reign a perpetual
truce.

Let us look to the tendency of the proposition,
that no custom-house shall be established at Fernando
Po, or at the post to be formed at the junction of the
Niger and the Tchadda : we might then hope that
the history of these stations would be a counterpart
to that of Singapore, which is described as having
been, in 1819, " an insignificant fishing-village, and
a haunt of pirates," but now stands as an eloquent
eulogy on the views of its founder, Sir Stamford
Raffles, proving what may be effected, and in how
short a time, for our own profit and for the improvement of the uncivilized world, " by the union of native
industry and British enterprise," when uncurbed by
restrictions on trade.

FREE LABOUR.

I now turn to the second great principle, viz.,— Free Labour.

It may be thought by some almost superfluous that this should be urged, considering that there is an Act of Parliament, which declares that " Slavery shall be, and is hereby utterly and for ever abolished *in all the* colonies, possessions, and plantations of Great Britain." But if ever there were a case in which this great law should be strictly and strenuously enforced, and in which it is at the same time peculiarly liable to be neglected or evaded, it is in the case of any possessions we may obtain in Africa. It is necessary to be wise in time, and never to suffer this baneful weed to take root there. Let us remember what it has cost us to extirpate it from our old colonies. It is remarkable that among the whole phalanx of antagonists to the abolition of West India Slavery, there was never one who was not, by his own account, an ardent lover of freedom. Slavery, in the abstract, was universally acknowledged to be detestable; and they were in the habit of pathetically deploring their cruel fate, and of upbraiding the mother-country, which had originally planted this curse among them; but property had entwined itself around the disastrous institution, and we had to contend with a fearful array of securities, marriage settlements, and vested interests of all kinds. Again, bondage, it was said, had seared the intellect, and

M 2

withered all that was noble in the bosoms of its victims. To have begun such an unrighteous system was an error, only less than that of suddenly eradicating it, and of clothing with the attributes of freemen, those whose very nature had been changed and defiled by servitude.

I firmly believe that much of all this was uttered in perfect sincerity ; and yet, I feel the most serious apprehensions lest these wholesome convictions should evaporate before the temptations of a country, where land of the richest fertility is to be had for 1d. per acre, and labourers are to be purchased for 4l. per head. We know, not only that the Portuguese are turning their attention to plantations in the neighbourhood of Loango, but that they have been bold enough to ask us to guarantee to them their property, that is their slaves, in these parts. This, together with certain ominous expressions which I have heard, convinces me that my apprehensions are not altogether chimerical ; and I am not sure that we shall not once more hear the antique argument, that Negroes, " from the brutishness of their nature," are incapable of being induced to work by any stimulus but the lash : at all events, we shall be assured, that if we attempt to establish Free Labour, we shall assail the prejudices of the African chiefs in the tenderest points. If we do not take care, at the outset, to render the holding of slaves by British subjects in Africa highly penal, and perilous in the last degree, we shall see British capital again embarked, and vested interest acquired in hu-

man flesh. We shall, in spite of the warning we
have had, commit a second time, the monstrous error,
to say nothing of the crime, of tolerating slavery.
A second time the slave-master will accuse us of
being at least accomplices in his guilt; and once
more we shall have to buy off opposition by an ex-
travagant grant of money.

The suggestion, then, that I make is that we shall
lay it down, as a primary and sacred principle, that
any man who enters any territory that we may
acquire in Africa, is from that moment " Free, and
discharged of all manner of slavery," and that Great
Britain pledges herself to defend him from all,
civilized or savage, who may attempt to recapture
him. That one resolution will do much to give us
labourers,—to obtain for us the affections of the population,—to induce them to imitate and adopt our
customs,—and to settle down to the pursuits of peaceful industry and productive agriculture.

No more daring attempt was ever made to form a
settlement in Africa than that undertaken by Captain
Beaver, near the close of the last century. His object
was to establish a colony on the island of Bulama.
Notwithstanding the errors into which he fell, and
which proved fatal to his expedition, yet was it
highly creditable to him, that at a time when the
abolition of the Slave Trade had made but little way
in the public mind, and when the extinction of slavery
was not thought of, he should have perceived, and
applied principles so wise and so humane as those we

find scattered in his interesting volume. His Narrative proves two points,—first, that the natives of Africa may be led to prefer legitimate commerce to slave-dealing. Secondly, that they were very willing to labour for wages.

The chief dissimilarity which first struck the Africans, in the conduct of this and that of other European settlements, was their refusal to purchase slaves.

" This they could not account for ; neither were they altogether pleased with it at first; for, when negotiating with Niobana for the purchase of the Biafara territory, he said, that ' It was very hard that we would not buy his slaves !' Having made him comprehend that our intention was rather to cultivate the earth than to trade; but that we should, notwithstanding, at all times, trade with him for wax, ivory, clothes, &c.,—in short, that we would buy everything which he had to sell, except only slaves, whom he could always dispose of as he had been accustomed to do heretofore—he appeared satisfied ; although he could not comprehend why we would not purchase the one, nor why we cultivated the other."

By their steadiness in this point, they got the character of being the first white men the natives had ever heard of " who could not do bad." And " from no circumstance," says Captain Beaver, " did we derive so much benefit, as from our not dealing in slaves."

The natives not long after found out that these new colonists not only refused to purchase slaves, but that no man in their settlement was permitted to be considered in the light of a slave. The two first who came to Captain Beaver were full of suspicion; they remained with him a little more than three weeks, and then signified their desire to depart at the time when their help was most needed. Captain Beaver wisely did not even ask them to remain, but paid them their wages, and dismissed them with presents. Their report induced others to take service, and he never after wanted grumetas : in one year, he employed nearly two hundred of them. The Africans of these parts always, he says, go armed, and never voluntarily place themselves in the power of even a friendly tribe; but when they had once ascertained that these English colonists neither bought nor sold slaves; that every man was paid for the full value of his labour, and suffered to depart whenever he chose, " They came to me unarmed," says Captain Beaver, "and remained for weeks and months at a time on the island, without the least suspicion of my ever intending them evil." And this, though he was occasionally obliged to inflict punishment on individuals of their number for disorderly conduct. " Thus," he says, " by the negative merit of treating these people with common integrity, was I not only able to acquire their confidence, and, by their labour, to do almost all that was done upon the island, but also to overturn one of their strongest prejudices against us, and to convert their well-grounded suspicion of fraud and deceit in all Europeans, into esteem and respect for the character of a white man."

I cannot dismiss the work of Captain Beaver, without expressing my satisfaction in finding, that he, like others whom I have named, gathers from his experience on the coast of Africa that the Slave Trade is to be overthrown by fair dealing, and by the wealth which is to be raised from the soil. " One great motive of the Africans in making slaves, indeed I may say the only one, is to procure European goods; slaves are the money, the circulating medium, with which African commerce is carried on : they have no other. If, therefore, we could substitute another, and at the same time that other be more certain and more abundant, the great object in trading in slaves will be done away. *This may be done by the produce of the earth.* " Let the native chiefs be once convinced that the labour of a free native in cultivating the earth may produce him more European goods in one year than he could have purchased if he had sold him for a slave, and he will no longer seek to make slaves to procure European commodities, but will cultivate the earth for that purpose." And this is the testimony which he bears to African industry, and to the facility of procuring labour :—

" I know that those who choose always to see the African character in its worst light will probably say that they never will be induced voluntarily to labour ; and that I betray a total ignorance of it, in supposing

that they can ever be brought to cultivate the earth
for wages.   That assertion may be made; but my
answer is, ' Put it to the test.'   And I moreover say
that, as far as my little knowledge of the Africans will
enable me to judge, I have no doubt of their readily
cultivating the earth for hire, whenever Europeans
will take the trouble so to employ them.   I never
saw men work harder, more willingly, or regularly,
generally speaking, than those free natives whom I
employed upon the island of Bulama.   What induced
them to do so?   Their desire of European commodities in my possession, of which they knew that they
would have the value of one bar at the end of a week,
or four at the end of a month.   Some of them
remained at labour for months ere they left me;
others, after having left me, returned: they knew
that the labour was constant, but they also knew that
their reward was certain.   I think, therefore, that
as far as my experience goes, I am warranted in
saying that the Africans are not averse to labour,
unless those in the neighbourhood of Bulama are
unlike the rest of their species.   So much as to the
question of labour."[*]

If I have quoted at unusual length from Captain
Beaver's work, it is because here is testimony upon
which no shade of suspicion can rest.   This work
was published before a word had been uttered upon
the controversy, as to free and slave labour; and it
comes from a gentleman who took nothing upon the

* Beaver's African Memoranda, p. 385.

authority of others, but formed his opinions from his own personal experience in Africa.

I shall subjoin in the Appendix further proof, on the authority of General Turner, Colonel Denham, and Major Ricketts, who also spoke from what they saw at Sierra Leone, as to the disposition of Africans to work for wages.*

The Rev. W. Fox, missionary at M'Carthy's Island, whom I have already quoted, says, " The Eastern Negroes, ... come here and hire themselves as labourers for several months, and, with the articles they receive in payment, barter them again on their way home for more than their actual value on this island." In the journal of the same gentleman, just received, under date of April, 1838, he writes thus : " I have to-day paid off all the labourers who had been employed on the mission-ground, and have hired about eighty more, with three overseers ; *many others applied for work*, and I should have felt a pleasure in engaging them, but that I wished to keep the expenses within moderate bounds."

It thus appears that free labour is to be obtained in Africa, even under present circumstances, if we will but pay the price for it, and that there is no necessity at all for that system of coerced labour, which no necessity could justify. I am aware that I have trespassed on the patience of many of my readers, who require no arguments against slavery ; but I have already expressed, and continue to feel, if there be

* Vide Appendix C.

danger anywhere in the plan for the cultivation of Africa, it lies in this point. And I wish the question of slavery to be definitively settled, and our principles to be resolved on, in such a way as shall render it impossible for us to retract them, before a single step is taken, or a shilling of property invested in the attempt to grow sugar and cotton in Africa.

I shall here introduce the consideration of two other points, which though they cannot precisely be classed as principles, yet are nearly akin to them, and deserve our very serious attention.

The proposal of a settlement in Africa, necessarily recalls to mind our vast empire in India ; and, surely, no sober-minded statesman would desire to see renewed, in another quarter of the globe, the career we have run in the East.

I entirely disclaim any disposition to erect a new empire in Africa. Remembering what has now been disclosed, of the affliction of that quarter of the globe, and of the horrors and abominations which every spot exhibits, and every hour produces, it would be the extreme of selfish cruelty to let a question so momentous be decided with an eye to our own petty interests ; but there is another view of the case,—it would also be the most extreme folly to allow ourselves to swerve one iota from its right decision, by any such indirect and short-sighted considerations.

What is the value to Great Britain of the sovereignty of a few hundred square miles in Benin, or Eboe, as compared with that of bringing forward into the market of the world millions of customers, who may be taught to grow the raw material which we require, and who require the manufactured commodities which we produce ? The one is a trivial and insignificant matter ; the other is a subject worthy the most anxious solicitude of the most accomplished statesmen.

It appears to me, however, that the danger of our indulging any thirst for dominion is rather plausible than real. In the first place, the climate there forbids the employment of European armies, if armies indeed formed any part of my plan, which they do not. I look forward to the employment, almost exclusively, of the African race. A few Europeans may be required in some leading departments ; but the great body of our agents must have African blood in their veins, and of course to the entire exclusion of our troops.

2dly. In Asia, there was accumulated treasure to tempt our cupidity : in Africa, there is none. Asia was left to the government of a company : the African establishments will, of course, be regularly subjected to parliamentary supervision. Our encroachments upon Asia were made at a time, when little general attention was bestowed, or sympathy felt, for the sufferings and wrongs of a remote people. Now, attention is awake on such topics. India stands as a beacon to warn us against extended dominion ; and if there were not, as I believe there are, better principles among our statesmen, there would be a check to rapacity, and a shield for the weak, in the wakeful commiseration of the public.

I may add, that, were the danger as great as some imagine, it would have disclosed itself ere this. The French have had for some time a settlement on the Senegal; the Danes on the Rio Volta; the Dutch on the Gold Coast; the Portuguese at Loango; the Americans at Cape Mesurado, and the English at Sierra Leone, in the Gambia, and on the Gold Coast; and I know not that there has been upon the part of any of these a desire manifested to raise an empire in Central Africa. Certainly, there has been none on the part of the British : on the contrary, I think there is some reason to complain that our government has been too slow, at least for the welfare of Africa, in accepting territory which has been voluntarily offered to us, and in confirming the treaties which have been made by our officers. We have been in possession of Sierra Leone not very far short of half a century ; and I am not aware that it can be alleged that any injury has been thereby inflicted upon the natives.

Lastly. There is this consideration, and to me it seems conclusive :—Granting that the danger to African liberty is as imminent as I consider it to be slight, still the state of the country is such, that, change as it may, it cannot change for the worse.

The other point to which I would call attention is, the encouragement which may be afforded to the infant cultivation of Africa, by promoting the admission and use of its productions. I shall not advert to the

assistance which we may fairly expect from the Le-
gislature in this respect, when the subject is brought
under its consideration in all its important bearings;
with the example of France and the United States
before them, I cannot doubt that Government will
introduce such measures as a liberal and enlightened
policy will dictate.   But individuals have it in their
power to contribute largely to the encouragement of
African produce, by a preference that will cost them
little.   Let them recollect that for centuries we were
mainly instrumental in checking cultivation in Africa:
we ransacked the whole continent in order to procure
labourers for the West Indies.   Is it, then, too much
to ask, now when we are endeavouring to raise her
from the gulf of wretchedness into which we have
contributed to plunge her, that while she is struggling
with enormous difficulties, we should force her industry and excite her to unfold her capabilities by
anxiously encouraging the consumption of her produce ?

CHAPTER VI.

ELEVATION OF NATIVE MIND.

———

" Wisdom is a defence, and money is a defence ; but the excellency of knowledge is, that Wisdom giveth Life to them that have it."—Ecclesiastes, vii. 12.
 " That peace and happiness, truth and justice, religion and piety, may be
established among them for all generations."—Liturgy.

———

I NOW come to the point which I deliberately consider to b beyond all others momentous in the question before us.   I lay great stress upon African commerce, *more* upon the cultivation of soil, but *most*
of all upon the elevation of the native mind.

This is a wide subject ; it embraces the consideration of some difficult questions.   They resolve themselves into these : 1st. Are the Africans able and
willing to learn ?   2d. *What,* and *how shall we teach*
them ?

It is true that the inhabitants of Africa are in the
very depths of ignorance and superstition ; but, still,
there are amongst them redeeming symptoms, however slight, sufficient to prove that the fault is not in
their nature, but in their condition ; and to teach us,
that when we shall have put down that prodigious evil
which forbids all hope of their improvement, it is abundantly possible that the millions of Africa may assume

their place among civilized and Christian nations ; and
that a region, whose rank luxuriance now poisons the
atmosphere, may be brought under subjection to the
plough, may yield a wealthy harvest to its occupants,
and open a new world, as exciting to our skill, capital,
and enterprise, as was America on its first discovery.
In these views it is a satisfaction to me that I can
lean upon an authority so stable as that of Mr. Pitt.
Mr. Wilberforce, writing to Mr. Stephen in 1817,
says : " Reflection renders me more and more confident that we shall, or, at least, that they who live a
few years will, see the beginnings of great reforms
in the West Indies, as well as *opening prospects of
civilization in Africa.*   In the latter instance I must
say, even to you, that Pitt's death has been an irre-
parable loss to us.   He had truly grand views on the
topic of our moral and humane debt to Africa." *
And there is a speech on record, of which Mr.
Sheridan said at the time, " If Mr. Pitt were always
thus to speak, the opposition could not survive a fortnight ;" and of which Mr. Fox said 15 years afterwards,
that it was " the most powerful eloquence that ever
adorned those walls ; a speech not of vague and showy
ornament, but of solid and irresistible argument ;" in
that speech Mr. Pitt said, " Some of us may live to
see a reverse of that picture, from which we now
turn our eyes with shame and regret ; we may live to
behold the natives of Africa engaged in the calm
occupations of industry, and in the pursuit of a just
and legitimate commerce ; we may behold the beams

* Wilberforce's Life, vol. iv. p. 306.

of science and philosophy breaking in upon their land, which, at some happier period, in still later times, may blaze with full lustre, and, joining their influence to that of PURE RELIGION, may illuminate and invigorate the most distant extremities of that immense continent."

In the first part of this work I have given a description of the deadly superstition which prevails in Africa, and of the effect it produces. The reader is requested to carry a sense of this most miserable state of things along with him, while we are considering what can be done towards the moral, intellectual, and religious improvement of the people.

Preliminary to this, I beg to call attention to cer· tain indications,—faint, no doubt,—but, considering the difficulties and impediments to improvement in Africa, encouraging indications,—of a capability for better things ;

And also, to show that there are facilities for giving instruction to the inhabitants, which hold out the hope that our labours, if we shall be induced to make them, will not be in vain.

Hence an argument for a mighty effort towards the moral and intellectual improvement of Africa, may be successfully derived.

Before I proceed to these indications of capability, I must premise that a just judgment cannot be formed of the Africans without reference to the circumstances in which they are placed. Things which would be no proof at all of intelligence in an European, who had

N

been taught the truths of religion, and been under
the influence of a certain measure of refinement and
civilization, denote positive intellect in an African
savage from his birth, imbibing the grossest superstition, and bereaved of motives to action by his insecurity.

What Allowance then should be made in favour of the Negro?

When we find that at this period of the world there
are nations not very remote from the centre of civilization, who have as yet learned the use of no agricultural implement but the hoe, and who, eager for
wealth, have not energy enough to till their land, or
work their mines, or in any way to avail themselves of
the prodigal bounty of nature, we are apt to rush to
the obvious but fallacious conclusion, that they are
not men in the ordinary sense of the term, but beings
of a stunted intellect, and of a degraded order.

This false conception has been the cause of infinite
suffering to the negro race. During the whole controversy on the subject of slavery, it was the great
defence and apology of the planters; it constituted
their whole case. They triumphantly pointed at the
idleness of the negro, and extracted from it a justifi-
cation of the *necessary* severity with which he was
treated. The error has not as yet been dissipated;
many benevolent persons, judging of the African
under his present aspect, despair of his improvement.

It will serve better than a thousand arguments to dispel this idea of inferiority in the African, and to induce us to make large allowances for him, notwithstanding his existing debasement, if I produce before my readers individuals of European extraction, of a race which amongst Europeans is supposed to stand in the highest rank for energy and intelligence, who have been, in the space of a few months, corrupted and debased by oppression. When Englishmen are masters, and Africans their slaves, we charge them with sloth, deception, thievishness ; and we rate them as another and an inferior order in the family of man. I am going to reverse the picture, and to show that when Africans are masters and Englishmen their slaves, they reckon us a poor, pitiful, degraded race of mortals ; inveterate thieves, and proverbial liars ; too lazy to work, too stupid to learn, too base to be credited ; hardly sensible of the obligation of an oath ; and fit only to be hewers of wood and drawers of water to the true believers, to whom God, in answer to their prayers, has been pleased to send them.

> " It may from many a blunder free us,
> To see ourselves as others see us."

Such, as I shall show, is the reproach in each case ; and in each case I doubt not that it is just. Let Slavery be imposed on man of whatever race, that man is found a poor, tame, degenerate creature. The black, being a slave, thieves ; so does the white. He lies ; so does the white. The black will not do a

N 2

stroke of work, except under the terror of the lash; just so the white. The fact, in both cases, is true; and the fallacy lies, not in an erroneous opinion of the demerits of the slave, but in this—that each forms his estimate on a being corrupted by oppression. He forgets that it is natural that the man reared in slavery should be tainted with slavish vices; that, denied access to knowledge, it is natural he should be ignorant; that, wanting a motive, he necessarily wants perseverance.

Before we can pronounce a man, or a race of men, desperately wicked, and incorrigibly idle, they must have their fair chances as men—we must give them a motive for their exertions. We must associate with the fatigues we call for, a sense of personal advantage to spring from them; we must awaken whatever there may be of native vigour sleeping in their bosoms, and we must release them from the trammels which incumber their progress, if we desire to see them advance with rapidity.

One corroboration of this doctrine is to be found in the history of Adams, who was wrecked upon the coast of Africa, made a slave to the inhabitants, and was carried to Timbuctoo. Adams was a British sailor. and our consul at Mogadore thus describes him at the termination of his captivity:—" *Like most other Christians, after a long captivity and severe treatment among the Arabs, he appeared, at his first arrival, exceedingly stupid and insensible.*"*

* Adams's Residence at Timbuctoo. Introd. p. 24.

But a still more forcible illustration of the truth of this theory is to be found in the very interesting narrative of the loss of the Oswego, on the coast of Africa, and the enslavement of Captain Paddock and his crew. He was a man on whose statement every reliance could be placed. De Witt Clinton, governor of New York, thus writes to him, October 1817,—" I have been urged by several respectable gentlemen, who, together with myself, repose the utmost confidence in your candour and veracity, and who have been a long time acquainted with the respectability of your standing in society, to solicit from you a statement of your sufferings and adventures." In compliance with this application, the narrative was published.

Captain Paddock was a Quaker, high in repute with the Society of Friends, by whom no man will be respected who is not strictly veracious. He himself gives proof of the effect which slavery had upon his own morals. He furnishes an elaborate description of his various modes of robbing and deceiving his master. He steals his corn, his tobacco, his fruit, his boat. He makes no scruple of telling falsehoods out of number to his master, and of purloining everything he could lay his hands on.

Of this, the following will serve as an illustration : —" I was soon after called away to furnish tobacco for a few who were smoking under the shade of the walls. When they had done, my second mate, who was as fond of tobacco as myself, suggested a query as to the propriety of robbing the pouch of a little.

We did so, and divided the spoil among such of our company as were tobacco-chewers. Not long after, some new company having come, I was again called upon to bring the pouch; and the fellow, on opening it, charged me with stealing from it. Against that charge I defended myself as well as I could. For some time I was unwilling to make the hazardous attempt again; but at last, while the Arabs were all lying asleep under the shade, I proposed to my second mate that we two should go off together to some distance, where we might have an opportunity of taking some out in such a manner as not to be suspected.

*   *   *   *   *

" We sat down in the finest piece of wheat I ever saw, and commenced the business that we went upon, taking particular notice of the turns of the string and knot of the pouch, in which, when we had unrolled it, we found two little sticks, laid in such a manner as to detect me in my next attempt upon it, and doubtless for that purpose. Having opened the tobacco, we took out as much of it as we durst, and replaced the little sticks as exactly as possible, when we rolled it up again, putting round it the string just as we found it, and hurried out of the field." *

The Africans having discovered that their captives were exceedingly idle, resorted to exactly our own methods of procuring (what was formerly so much dwelt upon in this country) " steady labour in the sun." They beat them, they starved them; they said to them, " If you will not work, neither shall

* Loss of the Oswego, p. 181.

you eat;" and even threatened to shoot them for
their indolence. Captain Paddock says, " Early in
the morning of the 27th, the sickles that the Arabs
brought with them were made ready, and all of us
were ordered out to work." This he refused, for
which he received their curses and threats, but determined not to heed them. " This controversy lasted
an hour, and they got my men into the field at last.
Some of them could handle a sickle as well as the
Arabs themselves ; and I told one of them (the man
that I was fearful would be of the most service to
our enslavers) to cut his own fingers, as if by accident. They all understood my meaning, and it was
not long after my men had been dragged into the
field before I found they were doing very well ;
I mean *well* for our own purposes. Some by accident, and some intentionally, perhaps, cut their
fingers and hands with their sickles, and made loud
complaints ; while others, who were gathering up
the grain for binding, did it in such a wasteful
manner, that their work was a real loss to the owner.
Upon this the Arabs took away the sickles from those
that had been reaping, and set them to haul the
grain up by the roots. They did so, but laid it in
the worst form that was possible. By managing
things in this way, they beat the Ishmaelites, and
got the victory."*

Their masters, finding that all their efforts to overcome the indolence of their Christian slaves were
ineffectual, directed their vengeance against Pad-

* Loss of the Oswego, p. 157 to 159.

dock, saying, " If Rias works, his men will, for he is
the head devil among them."

It is curious to remark that the opinions the Africans entertained of us bore a strong resemblance to
the doctrine, now I trust obsolete, but not long ago
in full vogue amongst ourselves, of the inferiority of
the African race.   All who took an interest in the
question of negro emancipation must remember the
deep prejudice which was felt by the white population of the West Indies against any approach towards
social intercourse with those who had black blood in
their veins.   I have heard of a clergyman who was
persecuted for admitting persons of colour to the
Sacrament at the same time with the whites; of a
gentleman who was banished from society for the
crime of permitting his own coloured daughters to
ride with him in his carriage through the public
streets; and upon the occasion of two gentlemen of
colour being admitted under the gallery of the House
of Commons when their own case was under discus-
sion, I heard a member of Parliament express in a
very animated speech his disgust at the insult thus
offered to the representatives of the people : " He had
hoped never to have seen the day when the laws of
decency and of nature might thus be trampled on."
We are not the only persons who have insisted on this
aristocracy of complexion.   Paddock and others have
recorded that " swinish-looking dogs and white-
skinned devils were the appellations which were fami-
liarly applied to them by Africans."   " The Arabs
were well received here ; but we were more ridiculed

than ever we had been, receiving an abundance of
the vile epithets so common to these people, who had
ever viewed us as a *poor degraded set of beings*,
scarcely fit to live in the world. The old man
(Ahomed) was seated opposite the gate at the time.
He spoke to me, and bade me sit down ; I sat down,
but, happening to sit near him, he ordered me away
to a greater distance, saying, he did not allow a Christian dog to be so near him ; I obeyed, and moved
off a little. The women were foremost in inso-
lence and abuse ; but their children were not far
behind them." * " They frequently spoke of us, but
in such a manner as often to remind me of the old
adage, ' Listeners seldom hear any good of themselves.' That saying was verified here completely.
The heads of their discourse concerning us were,†

* Loss of the Oswego, page 208.

† About the same estimate of negroes was at one time entertained by British subjects. " An Act for the Security of the
Subject" was passed in Bermuda in 1730. A passage of it runs
thus :—"Whereas, they (negroes, Indians, mulattos) being, for
brutishness of their nature, no otherwise valued or esteemed
amongst us than as our goods and chattels, or other personal
estates ; be it therefore enacted, that if any person or persons
whatsoever, within these islands, being owner or possessor of any
negroes, Indians, mulattos, or other slaves, shall, in the deserved
correction or punishment of his, her, or their slave or slaves, for
crimes or offences by them committed or supposed to be committed,
accidentally happen to kill any such slave or slaves, the aforesaid
owner or possessor shall not be liable to any imprisonment, arraign-
ment, or subject to any penalty or forfeiture whatsoever ; but if
any person or persons whatsoever shall *maliciously and wilfully*
kill and destroy any slave or slaves, then the aforesaid person or

that we were a poor, miserable, degraded race of mortals, doomed to the everlasting punishment of hell fire after death, and, in this life, fit only for the company of dogs; that our country was so wretchedly poor that we were always looking out abroad for sustenance, and ourselves so base as to go to the coast of Guinea for slaves to cultivate our land, being not only too lazy to cultivate it ourselves, but too stupid to learn how to do it; and finally, that if all Christians were to be obliged to live at home, their race would soon be extinct;" and "an old man swore that we were not worthy of a mouthful of bread."* " They think that there are no people in the world so active and brave as themselves, nor any so well informed; and they proudly say that they are at war with all the world, and fear nobody." †

Upon one occasion, the Arab appears to have had the best of the argument. " Ahomed made some inquiries of me respecting the manufactories of my own country, which I answered as well as I could; and I took the liberty to tell him how much better he would be treated than we had been, if by any accident he should be thrown on our shores; that, in such an event, instead of being held in bondage, and sold from tribe to tribe, our súltan would have him conducted back to his native country in safety. He heard me out, and then warmly retorted upon me as follows :—' You say, if I were in your country, your

persons shall forfeit and pay unto our Sovereign Lord the King the full sum of ten pounds current money."

* Loss of the Oswego, p. 148.　　　　† Ibid. 144.

people would treat me better than I treat you. There is no truth in you. If I were there, I should be doomed to perpetual slavery, and be put to the hardest labour in tilling your ground. You are too lazy to work yourselves in your fields, and therefore send your ships to the negro coast, and, in exchange for the useless trinkets with which you cheat the poor negroes, you take away ship-loads of them to your country, from which never one returns; and had your own ship escaped our shore, you yourself would now be taking the poor negroes to everlasting slavery.'

" Although the purpose of my voyage had been very different from what Ahomed suspected, yet I felt the sting of this reproach in a manner that I can never forget."

Upon another occasion, Ahomed drew no very flattering comparison between the conduct of Christians and that of the followers of the Prophet. " The negroes are men that you Christian dogs have taken from the Guinea country, a climate that suits them best. You are *worse than Arabs*, who enslave you only when it is God's will to send you to our coast. Never, I must confess, did I feel a reproach more sensibly."*

The distinction made by the Arab between the conduct of Mussulmans and Christians, was as just as it was ingenious. Their creed permits the disciples of the true Prophet to enslave the heretics; whereas, our purer faith says, " Whatsoever ye would that men should do to you, do ye even so to them;" and

* Loss of the Oswego, p. 112.

abounds in noble passages, denouncing God's wrath against the oppressor, and particularly that oppressor who is a man-stealer, and " who taketh his neighbour's labour without wages, and giveth him nought for his work."

We remember the time when a negro slave who absconded was convicted and punished as a thief. He had run away with his master's chattels, *i. e.* his own body. The Arab seems to have adopted a somewhat similar train of reasoning. " After a few minutes' silence," says Captain Paddock, " Ahomed accosted me in the following manner :—' *There is no confidence to be placed in Christians ;* for whenever they come ashore on our coast, they bury their money in the sand, as you yourself have done, to prevent it from falling into the hands of the true believers. *It is our property.* We pray earnestly to the Almighty God to send Christians ashore here : he hears our prayers, and often sends us good ships ; and if you did as you ought to do, we should have the benefit of them."*

It is very curious that, in the course of their journey, they fell in with a tribe of African abolitionists and Mahommedan quakers.. At one town their reception was different to what it had usually been. " I inquired," said Paddock, "who they were. He replied, ' They belong to a sect called *Foulah.* They will not mix with the other inhabitants, but choose to live altogether by themselves ; and are so stupid, that if the Emperor of Morocco should march

* Loss of the Oswego, p. 190.

an army to cut off the whole race, they would not defend themselves, but would die like fools, as they are.' I asked him if they used fire-arms. ' No,' said he, ' they make no use of them; and if God was pleased to send a Christian ship ashore near them, they would neither seize upon the goods nor the men, nor would they buy a slave of any kind.' I asked him if they were numerous; and he answered, ' No, they are not numerous; but the dwellings you see on the sides of the hills yonder are theirs, and in many other places they are to be found; and wherever they are, they always keep together by themselves.' Finally, I asked him if they were Mahometans. ' Yes,' he answered, ' they are, or else we would destroy them; but they are poor ignorant dogs, and little better than the Christians.' "*

I should feel myself called upon to apologise to my readers for these lengthened quotations, were it not important to show that Europeans and Christians are not proof against that moral poison which belongs to oppression. Let a man, European, American, or African, imbibe that taint, and its virulence will be manifest in the stupidity of his understanding, in the deadness of his moral sense; it will be visible to the eye of the most careless observer, even in the external features and carriage of its victim. Reduced to the condition of a slave, he will droop and relax, and become good for nothing, or next to nothing. We see that a race fortified by early association, by the resources of intellect and education, and by the elevating prin-

* Loss of the Oswego, p. 199.

ciples of Christianity, placed in precisely the same
circumstances as the African, exhibits precisely the
same degree of degeneracy. And can we wonder
that they who have so long been the victims of every
species of cruelty, should not as yet have put forth
those generous qualities and that higher order of intellect which will not grow, except in a genial atmosphere, and on a favouring soil ? Does not this rescue
the African from the supposed stigma of inferiority ?

Franklin defines a slave to be " an animal who eats
as much, and works as little, as possible." The
black, the brown, the red, the white races of men,
are alike indolent when they want a motive for exertion.   " Ye be idle, ye be idle," was the reproach of
Pharaoh to his Israelitish bondsmen; " ye be idle,
ye be idle," says the master to the slave in all nations
and in all ages.

> " 'T is liberty alone that gives the flow'r
> Of fleeting life its lustre and perfume,
> And we are *weeds* without it.

I now proceed to the enumeration of the symptoms
which lead me to hope that in due time the African
races may be excited to industry, ingenuity, and
perseverance.

I admit that on the coast there is a belt of slave-
trading chiefs, who, at present, find it more profitable to supply the slave-markets than to conduct
a legitimate commerce. Little business can be done
when there are any slavers at their stations,—indeed,
the fair traders are always compelled to wait until
the human cargoes are completed. These chiefs

not only obstruct the fair trader on the coast,
but as much as possible prevent his access to the
interior.   Insecurity, demoralisation, and degradation are the results; but as we recede from the
coast, and ascend the rivers, comparative civilisation is
found, industry becomes apparent, and no inconsiderable skill in many useful arts is conspicuous.   All
travellers have observed the superior cultivation, and
comparatively dense population of the inland regions.
Laird, in ascending the Niger, writes, " Both banks
of the river are thickly studded with towns and villages; I could count seven from the place where we
lay aground; and between Eboe and the confluence of
the rivers, there cannot be less than 40, one generally
occurring every two or three miles.   The principal
towns are Attah and Addakudda; and averaging the
inhabitants at 1,000, will, I think, very nearly give
the population of the banks.   *   *   *   The
general character of the people is much superior to
that of the swampy country between them and the
coast.   They are shrewd, intelligent, and quick in
their perception, milder in their disposition, and
more peaceable in their habits."   Oldfield says
(vol. i. p. 163,) that, from the great number of towns
they passed, he is inclined to suppose that the population must be very dense indeed.   And (vol. ii. p.
17,) " no sooner does the traveller approach one town,
than he discovers three or four, and sometimes five
others."   Park speaks (vol. ii. p. 80,) of the " hills
cultivated to the very summit, and the surplus grain
employed in purchasing luxuries from native traders."

Laing speaks (p. 156) with delight of " the extensive meadows, clothed in verdure, and the fields from which the springing rice and ground-nuts were sending forth their green shoots, not inferior in beauty and health to the corn-fields of England, interspersed here and there with a patch of ground studded with palm-trees." Tuckey reports (p. 342) a similar improvement in the face of the country at some distance up the Congo, where he found towns and villages following each other in rapid succession. Ashmun, writing from Liberia, says, " An excursion of some of our people into the country, to the distance of about 140 miles, has led to a discovery of the populousness and comparative civilisation of this district of Africa, never till within a few months even conjectured by myself. We are situated within 50 leagues of a country, in which a highly improved agriculture prevails; where the horse is a common domestic animal, where extensive tracts of land are cleared and enclosed, where every article absolutely necessary to comfortable life is produced by the skill and industry of the inhabitants; where the Arabic is used as a written language in the ordinary commerce of life; where regular and abundant markets and fairs are kept; and where a degree of intelligence and practical refinement distinguishes the inhabitants, little compatible with the personal qualities attached, in the current notions of the age, to the people of Guinea." *

The wants of the people in Africa must not, any more than their industry and enterprise, be judged of

* From Miss. Regr. for 1828, p. 335.

by what is observable on the coast. The Moors, who have preceded us in the interior, have imparted more knowledge of commercial transactions than we may suppose. Captain Clapperton told Mr. Hamilton that he could have negotiated a bill on the Treasury of London at Soccatoo. The Moors have introduced the use of the Arabic in mercantile affairs; and that language is nearly as useful in Africa, as the French language is in Europe. In 1812, Mr. Willis, formerly British Consul for Senegambia, stated his belief that in the warehouses of Timbuctoo were accumulated the manufactures of India and Europe, and that the immense population of the banks of the Niger are thence supplied. A Moorish merchant reported to Mr. Jackson, that between Mushgrelia and Houssa there were more boats employed on the river than between Rosetta and Cairo ; and that the fields of that country were enclosed and irrigated by canals and water-wheels,*—a demonstrative proof of the activity, industry, and civilisation of the people.

" Thirty years' experience," says an African merchant (Mr. Johnston), " of the natives, derived from living amongst them for the whole of that period, leaves a strong impression on my mind that, with due encouragement, they would readily be led to the cultivation of the soil, which I think in most places capable of growing anything."   Mr. Laird, in a letter to me, observes,—" As to the character of the inhabitants, I can only state that, if there is one characteristic

* Jackson's Timbuctoo, pp. 24, 38, and 427.

o

that distinguishes an African from other uncivilised people, it is his love of, and eagerness for, traffic : men, women, and children trade in all directions. They have regular market-places where they bring the produce of their fields, their manufactures, their ivory, and everything they can sell. * * * At the Iccory-Market I have seen upwards of one hundred large canoes, each holding from ten to forty men, all trading peaceably together. I was informed by the natives that it was considered neutral ground, and that the towns at war with one another, attended the same market amicably." The industrious inhabitants of the Grain Coast supply Sierra Leone, and Liberia with the greatest portion of their food.

One of the sub-agents of the Slave Trading Company, which I have already noticed, thus writes to his principal from the town of Gotto, about ten leagues up the river Benin, of date 20th June, 1837 : " I was astonished to see so large a market the day I arrived.   The town is large and eligible ; there were at least 4000 persons at market with all sorts of commodities for sale."

Of their capabilities of improvement we may judge from the rude efforts of negroes transported from North America, or liberated from slave-ships at Sierra Leone.   What these men have wanted, as Colonel Denham remarks, is " instruction, example, and capital ;" and he adds, " that, with the small amount of either that they have received, it is a sub-

* Class A, 1838-9, p. 64.

ject of astonishment to him that they have done what they have."—(Despatch, 21st May, 1829.) They supply the market of Freetown with plenty of fruit and vegetables, such as yams, cassada, Indian corn, ground-nuts, pine-apples, sugar-canes, &c., &c.

Nearly the same account may be given of the exuberant fertility of the eastern as of the western coast, and of the lucrative character of the commerce which might be there carried on were it not for the destructive Slave Trade. I have been informed by the captain of a merchant-vessel who was long on the eastern coast, that before the Slave Trade absorbed the whole attention of the people, two merchant-ships used to be annually despatched from Lisbon, which for the most paltry outfit, brought home return cargoes of from 40,000*l.* to 60,000*l.**

Other testimonies might be added to show that the African is not wanting in those qualities which accompany civilisation, and he only requires that a right direction should given to his industry and intelligence, to qualify him for intercourse with the more refined European.

* The gentleman who furnished this information, mentions the following articles of commerce on the eastern coast of Africa:— Gold, silver, copper, iron, ivory, horns, tallow, hides, skins, tortoiseshell, ostrich-feathers, pearls, ambergris, amber, gums and various drugs, palm-oil, cocoa-nut oil, black whale-oil, sperm-oil, bees'-wax in great abundance, coffee, tobacco, indigo, corn, rice, &c. A most profitable trade might also be carried on in cowries, which abound on the coast, where he has purchased them at 4*d.* a-bushel; on the western coast they are the current coin, and are told out by the hundred. All these articles find a ready market at Ceylon, Bombay, and Calcutta.

The eagerness with which the Timmanees entered into the laborious and fatiguing work of cutting, squaring, and floating to the trading stations the immense bodies of heavy teak timber exported from Sierra Leone, is a convincing proof of their readiness to engage in any employment where they can get a reward, however small, for their labour. It is well known that during the time the timber trade was in activity, several native towns were formed on the banks of the river, and many natives came from a distance up the country to engage in it. Timber was cut at the termination of the largest creeks at Port Logo, and even so far as Rokou, and floated down to Tombo, Bance Island, and Tasso. (Laing, p. 77.)*

I have lately seen a portion of the Journal of the Rev. W. Fox, written at Macarthy's Island, in which, of date September 3, 1836, he mentions having given away a considerable number of Arabic Scriptures to Mandingoes, and to Serrawoollies, or Tiloboonkoes, as they are here more generally termed; which literally means Eastern people, as they come from the neighbourhood of, and beyond, Bondou, and are strict Mahommetans. They come here and hire themselves

* " Twenty years ago," says Laird (vol. ii. p. 363), " African timber was unknown in the English market. There are now from 13,000 to 15,000 loads annually imported. In 1832 Mr. Forster, in a letter to Lord Goderich, stated the importation as high as ' from 15,000 to 20,000 loads, giving employment to 20,000 tons of shipping annually.' From 3,000 to 4,000 loads of red teak-wood are exported annually from the Gambia," and the mahogany from that river is now much used for furniture.

as labourers for several months, and with the articles they receive in payment barter them again on their way home for more than their actual value on this island.

The Kroomen who inhabit Cape Palmas are a most extraordinary race of men. They neither sell nor allow themselves to be made slaves. These men leave their homes young, and work on board the trading vessels on the coast, or at Sierra Leone Their attachment to their country is great, nor will they engage themselves for more than three years. "To my mind," says Mr. Laird, in the letter to me which I have before quoted, "these men appear destined by Providence to be the means of enabling Europeans to penetrate into the remotest parts of Africa by water. They are patient, enduring, faithful, easily kept in order, and brave to rashness when led by white men. Any number may be got at wages from two to four dollars per month."

We thus find that little difficulty exists in procuring either labourers or seamen in Africa.

To those disposed to make the necessary allowances, it is something to know that it has been remarked by many travellers, that the Africans are by no means devoid of aptitude and ingenuity in imitating European manufactures. Thus, at the island of Tombo Mr. Rankin* saw the lock of a rifle which had been so well repaired by a Foulah, who had never seen any but the fractured one, that strict examina tion was necessary to discover what part had been

* Rankin, vol. i. p. 130.

replaced. In Benin they make muskets, procuring only the locks from Europe; and at the market of Jennè, De Caillie observed gunpowder, of an inferior kind indeed to ours, but of home manufacture. In most parts of Africa the natives have some notion of working metals.* They are acquainted with many dyes, and make much use of indigo. Colonel Denham† says that the dark blue of the tobes (or tunic) worn in Bornou cannot be excelled in any part of the world; and Kano is famed for its indigo establishments. I am told that they are also acquainted with a plant which produces a more brilliant blue than the indigo. From other vegetable substances they obtain other colours; thus Wadstrom stated to the Committee of 1790,‡ that the whole army of the king of Damel was clothed in cloth of native manufacture, dyed orange and brown. They also give a red or black dye to their leather; for the tanning of which they use several kinds of bark.§

In the year 1818 Mr. Clarkson had a conference, on the subject of the Slave Trade, with the Emperor Alexander at Aix-la-Chapelle. I have before me a private letter which he wrote to J. J. Gurney, Esq., describing the interview. He states that he exhibited articles in leather, in iron, in gold, in cotton cloth, mats, &c. " Having gone over all

* The Rev. Mr. Fox has recently presented me with two gold rings of excellent workmanship, manufactured by a native of the Gambia.

† Clapperton, p. 60.

‡ Abbrev. Evid. vol. iii. p. 10.

§ Rankin, vol. i. p. 132. Clapperton, p. 61, 62.

the articles, the Emperor desired me to inform him whether he was to understand that these articles were made by the Africans in their own country, that is, in their own native villages; or after they had arrived in America, where they would have an opportunity of seeing European manufactures. I replied, that such articles might be found in every African village, both on the coast and in the interior; and that they were samples of their own ingenuity, without any connection with Europeans. ' Then,' said the Emperor, ' you have given me a new idea of the state of these poor people. I was not aware that they were so far advanced in society. The works you have shown me are not the works of brutes, but of men endued with rational and intellectual powers, and capable of being brought to as high a degree of proficiency as other men. Africa ought to be allowed to have a fair chance of raising her character in the scale of the civilised world.' I replied that it was the cruel traffic which had prevented her from rising to a level with other countries, and that it was really astonishing to me that the natives had, under its impeding influence, arrived at the perfection which displayed itself in the specimens he had just seen. The Emperor replied that it was equally astonishing to him, for that wherever the trade existed, a man could have no stimulus to labour; being subject every hour to be taken away for a slave, he could not tell whether he should enjoy the fruits of it; he was sure upon this principle that no man in Africa would sow more corn than was sufficient for his own consumption;

and so the same principle would prove an obstacle to
any extraordinary cultivation of the works of art."

The natives have some turn both for husbandry and
gardening.   In the more settled parts of the interior
more pains are taken with cultivation, and even the
slaves are said to work better than those on the coast.
One of the best specimens of African agriculture is
given by De Caillie, as observed by him at Kimba, on
the road between Kankan and Jennè :—

" I walked about in the neighbourhood of our
habitation, and was delighted with the good cultivation; the natives raise little mounds of earth in which
they plant their pistachios and yams; and these
mounds are arranged with some taste, all of the same
height, and in rows.   Rice and millet are sown in
trenches; as soon as the rainy season commences, they
put in the seed around their habitations, and when
the maize is in flower they plant cotton between the
rows.   The maize is ripe very early, and they then
fill it up to make room for the other crop.   If they
do not plant cotton, they turn up the ground after the
maize is got in, and transplant the millet into it, a
practice which I never observed in Kankan.   I was
surprised to find these good people so laborious and
careful; on every side in the country I saw men and
women weeding the fields.   They grow two crops
in the year on the same land; I have seen rice in
ear, and other rice by its side scarcely above the
ground."*

Agriculture is obviously one of the first arts to

* De Caillie's Travels, vol. i. p. 293, 294.

which we ought to direct their attention, not merely as furnishing the surest ground for our future commercial intercourse, but as tending to bring the people into a condition of life most favourable for the reception and spread of Christianity. When Mr. Read set forth to convert the Bushmen on the frontier of Cape colony, he is reported to have said, " We take a plough with us ; but let it be remembered, that in Africa the Bible and the plough go together." And in the same spirit should I desire that our operations might be carried on. At present, indeed, trade (the barter of such articles as the country spontaneously produces, and which may suffice for the limited demand Africa has hitherto known,) is likely to be more to their taste than an occupation requiring regular labour ; still the cultivation which has arisen in many places on the stoppage of the Slave Trade, the groundnuts grown for sale on the Gambia, the corn raised for exportation on the Gold Coast, the cutting of timber at Sierra Leone, and the preparation of palm-oil at the mouths of the Niger, prove that these people may be led to adopt new methods of earning wealth by honest industry. In fact I think it is evident that, as Sir R. Mends wrote in 1823 to the Admiralty, " wherever the traffic in slaves has been checked, the natives have shown a fair and reasonable desire for cultivating the productions of their country."*

* It is impossible not to observe with regret how little these " desires " have met with encouragement from Europeans. Captain Arabin, in describing the fertile banks of the river Cassamanza, where the Portuguese have factories, thus refers to the

The negro's aptitude for letters has, as we may well suppose, been still less exercised than his manual skill; but we have proof, I think, that as a race, they are by no means deficient. On this point I may quote the words of an accurate observer, a Quaker lady,* who devoted much of her life to the promotion of African education, and at last sacrificed it in the cause.

" If my heart might speak from what my eye has seen, I would say I am fully convinced that it is not any inferiority in the African mind, or natural capacity, that has kept them in so depressed a state in the scale of society, but the lack of those advantages which are, in the usual order of Providence, made use of as instruments for the advancement and improvement of human beings. Those disadvantages which they, in common with other uncivilised natives, have suffered, have with them been cruelly increased, by that oppression, which, wherever exercised, has a natural ten-inhabitants, who, though now hardly to be distinguished from the aboriginal negroes, yet are partly descended from the first settlers. " They have remarkably fine cotton and indigo, and manufacture from them cloth of a dye and texture highly esteemed in Africa, and susceptible of much greater improvement; but the Portuguese, neglecting these advantages and capabilities of a people who have a mixture of their own blood in their veins, direct their attention almost wholly to the traffic in slaves, and sell indiscriminately these ingenious artificers, with their wives and children, whenever they can catch them."—" State of the Slave Trade," in the *Amulet*, 1832, p. 218.

* Hannah Kilham, who made three voyages to Africa for the sake of acquainting herself with the native languages ; she reduced to writing the Wolof or Jaloof, in which she printed reading lessons.

dency to fetter, to depress, and to blunt the powers
of the mind; and it is very unfair, and a great aggravation of the cruelty, to reflect on the victims of it, as
wanting ability for any other station than that which
they have been suffered to fill. I do not think that
even here [Sierra Leone] Africans have had a fair
trial of what they might be, had they the same advantages in education, and circumstances connected with
education, which Europeans have been favoured with,
yet their intelligent countenances, and the ability they
show when rightly instructed, evince certainly no
deficiency in the natural powers of the mind; they
come here, as to a foreign land, the language of
which is quite strange and unknown to them, they are
taught in this strange language, (those of them who
have school instruction,) from lists of detached words,
spelling lessons, many of which they never hear but
in those lessons, and their meaning therefore remains
unknown."*

"It seems very evident from what we hear, that
civilisation is prevented, or has been prevented, along
the coast, by the prevalence of the horrid traffic in
men; and the interior, north of the line, is much more
civilised than near the coast. The interior of the
south appears to be little known. I wish the sceptical as to African capacity could have seen a Foulah
man, of striking and intelligent countenance, who was
here the other day, and have heard his melodious
reading of Arabic manuscripts. I am informed, both
here and in the Gambia, that the Mahomedans of

* Letter from H. Kilham to W. Allen, 1824.

Western Africa are the most orderly and well conducted part of the African population. Their zeal
in the promotion of Arabic schools should stimulate
Europeans of higher profession. If persons be suit-
ably introduced, so as that their designs are fully
known, I believe intercourse, where only good is
intended, would, in most places, be made more easy
than some are willing to believe." *

FACILITIES FOR GIVING INSTRUCTION.

There is no more encouraging feature than the
readiness which has been generally observed on the
part of the negroes, to obtain for their children, and
sometimes for themselves, the advantages of education. Their love of acquiring knowledge, especially
that of languages, is thus spoken of by Mr. Laird.

" The eagerness with which the Africans thirst
after knowledge, is a very striking feature in their
character; on the coast great numbers have learned
to read writing from the captains of merchant vessels."†
He mentions that the late Duke Ephraim, chief of
Old Calabar, though he could not read a newspaper,
yet considered it essential to have a supply of books.
" The schools at Sierra Leone and Cape Coast have
done most, if not all, the good that has been done. I
know an instance now of a captured slave, resident
at Fernando Po, who sent his son to England for
education. All the chiefs would gladly pay for the

* Appendix to Second Report of African Instruction Society,
p. 11.
† Laird, vol. ii. p. 395.

board and education of their children. In the interior, in every village where Mahommedanism is professed, the children crowd to learn to mutter Arabic prayers and scraps of the Koran."

Liberia presents the example of a black community managing their own affairs on civilised principles. There, besides the governor, there is scarcely a white man in authority. They have two public libraries, a press, and the journal of the colony, "The Liberian Herald," is edited by a negro, the son of a slave of Virginia, and frequently contains able dissertations written by men of the same race.

Mr. Ashmun found the natives bordering on the American Colony of Liberia very desirous of putting their children under his care. He writes in a Report, 1825:—" No man of the least consideration in the country, will desist from his importunities until at least one of his sons is fixed in some settler's family.*

At this time many of the natives reside in the colony, and are gradually adopting the habits of civilised life. Many came thither for the express purpose of obtaining a Christian education, for which purpose, also, many of the native kings continue to send their sons. Missionaries of various denominations have penetrated into the neighbouring states, and all have sent cheering accounts of their success and prospects.†

* Life of Ashmun, p. 271.

† Address of Judge Payne to the Vermont Colonisation Society, 1838.

Two Wesleyan ministers, Messrs. Dove and Badger, visited the " Plantains," an island on the mouth of the 'Sherbro', in April, 1839.

Mr. Dove says, " The island has a beautiful appearance, and the cattle on it look as fine as any I ever saw in my native land. The island, though small, belongs to King Calker, who treated us with great kindness. We took up our abode in the royal apartments, and the next day we dined with his Majesty. He is certainly a sensible man, and seems to be quite free from the vile and superstitious customs practised throughout the ' Sherbro' country; he possesses a pretty good knowledge of English, and expressed a wish to have a missionary to live with him; we had the high gratification of seeing him reading an English Bible. His brother, also, is a sincere inquirer after truth: having received some instruction when young, and living in Freetown, he now instructs both children and adults, and when we witnessed the result of this king's brother's labour, we could not but rejoice. He has translated several portions of the sacred Scriptures, catechisms, and some of our excellent hymns, into the ' Sherbro' language : he wishes me, if possible, to get them printed for the use of the heathen around him."

Besides this eagerness on the part of the African tribes to obtain intellectual and useful instruction, there is also a most encouraging willingness to receive, and listen to, the teachers of Christianity. Indeed, I am not aware of any instance of Christian teachers having been repelled, when their object has been fairly understood, except, indeed, by the notorious influence of European Slave Traders. These miscreants obliged the church missionaries to leave some of their stations; an event deeply to be regretted, as they had established some excellent schools on the Rio Pongas: one of their scholars was Simeon Wilhelm, who died in England in 1817, and was well known as a young man of remarkable promise.*

Within the last three years Mr. Fox has visited the chiefs of Woolli, Bondou, Barra, and Nyani, and obtained from all, Pagan and Mahomedan, invitations for missionaries. The following is the account he gives of an interview with Saada, the Almamy of Bondou.

On Saturday, April 28, 1838, Mr. Fox reached Boollibanny, the capital of the Mahomedan state of Bondou, and on the following day had an interview with Saada, who was encamped six miles from the city, and was about to start on a marauding expedition. On being introduced, Mr. Fox immediately stated the object of his journey, adding that he had visited the kingdoms of Barra, Nyani, and Woolli, and that those kings were favourable to his design; and giving, at the Almamy's request, a brief summary of the doctrines and precepts of Christianity. The Almamy replied, that all that had been said was very good; and that Mr. Fox might look at the Bondou

* See the Life of Wilhelm, by the Rev. Mr. Bickersteth.

ground, and inform him when he had fixed upon a
place ; but that he and his people must still follow
Mahomet.

" This being ended," Mr. Fox continues, " I told
him I had one request to make ; namely, that he
would abandon the war he had in contemplation.
In reply to my request, the Almamy asked, Why I
did not wish him to go to war?   I answered, From
the misery that must of necessity follow ; but especially because of the Divine command given to
Moses, ' Thou shalt do no murder.'   Shortly after
this, I shook hands with this powerful chief, and we
returned to our lodgings at Boollibanny.

" About an hour afterwards, to my surprise and
that of others, the Almamy and his war-tribe came
galloping home."

Mr. Freeman's visit to Ashantee has been already
noticed.   On this occasion his converts gave proof of
the effect of the gospel which he had preached to them.
No nation could have been more barbarously treated by
another, than the Fantees by the Ashantees ; who
had exercised their power in the most ferocious manner, not only slaying them by thousands in the field,
and destroying their villages, but putting hundreds of
them to death by torture.   It has been only British
protection that has preserved the weaker race ; yet
no sooner did the ill-used Fantees hear of Mr. Freeman's views than they entered fully into them, and
became, as he says, " not only willing, but anxious
for him to go up to Coomassie."   Such a salutary

feeling has religion wrought in them, that they are now making a voluntary subscription to send the gospel to their blood-thirsty enemies.

We have also seen the results of Mr. Freeman's evpedition; the impression made upon his mind was thus stated by himself after his return. " I am happy to inform you, that through the mercy of the God of missions, I have surmounted every difficulty, and returned fully satisfied that even the sanguinary Ashantees are ready to receive the gospel, and that, as soon as the committee can send a good supply of missionaries to this station, we shall, by the blessing of God, establish a mission among that people." *

In their last report, the Church Missionary Society state that they also hope soon to be able to extend their operations from Sierra Leone into the interior, that some preliminary excursions had been made by the missionaries, and that *the reception they met with from the people was encouraging*.

AGENTS TO BE OBTAINED.

We have already seen the desirableness of educating and civilising the inhabitants of Africa; and a number of facts have been brought to light, tending to show, that there is at least as great a readiness on their part to receive instruction, as on ours to communicate it; the question now remains—Who are to be the instructors? The climate is generally viewed as unfavourable to Europeans, and this being

* Wesleyan Missionary Notices, November, 1839, p. 166.

the case, I have great satisfaction in finding, that from among the liberated Africans in our West Indian Colonies, we are likely to be furnished with a number of persons, in whom are united the desirable qualifications of fitness for the climate, competency to act as teachers, and willingness to enter upon the work.

An important feature of the present time is this, that the exertions of the missionaries in the West Indies are beginning to tell on their converts in the missionary spirit which they have imparted. There is a feeling in the hearts of our emancipated negroes towards the land of their origin, which seems to have arisen spontaneously in various congregations.

Last December, in the hope that openings might ere long occur for the employment of native agents, I addressed, through the Rev. Mr. Trew, a circular to the heads of missionary societies, inquiring whether trustworthy persons could be found for various departments of our operations. Before answers could be received, the Rev. Mr. Dyer, the secretary of the Baptist Missionary Society, transmitted to me an inquiry on their part in the following letter to the committee at home, from the minister of one of their congregations in Jamaica.

Montego Bay, Jan. 21st, 1839.

" We beg to press upon your attention a subject of vast importance, and shall feel thankful if, at the very earliest opportunity, you will bring it before the members of the committee, with our earnest request that they will take it into their prayerful and serious consideration, and without delay adopt measures to realise the desires of many thousands of their fellow Christians in this island. The subject is, a mission to the interior of Western Africa; the land from which the beloved people of our charge, or their forefathers, were stolen, and which is at present without the light of the gospel, and suffering under accumulated wrongs. We, their ministers, feel on this subject an intense interest, while in *their* hearts the strongest emotions are excited for the perishing land of their fathers. The conversion of Africa to God is the theme of their conversation and their prayers, and the object of their most ardent desires. For this they are willing to toil, and devote the fruits of their labour, while some are anxious to go themselves, and proclaim to their kindred the love of Christ in dying for their salvation. In short, a feeling prevails among the members of our churches, to check which would be to injure their piety, and we believe would grieve that Divine Spirit, by whose gracious influences those feelings have been excited.

"There being no direct communication between this island and Africa, and few sources of information respecting that country being opened to us, we are at a loss to fix upon any plan to carry our desires into effect, and are therefore desirous that the committee should give it all the consideration it demands, and as early as possible communicate their sentiments to us."

The following letter to myself, from a highly respectable gentleman, is of a somewhat similar character :—

Kingston, Jamaica, May 1st, 1839.

" It is very remarkable that before being acquainted with the movements in England, *we* had been acting in some measure practically on your principle. Three or four months ago a large meeting, consisting of betwixt 2000 and 3000 persons, was held in this city, for the purpose of considering the best means of Christianising Africa, by such Christian agency as we could collect in this island. I was president of that meeting, and on my return home, what was my surprise to find upon my table Mr. Trew's circular, inquiring to what extent a Christian commercial agency for operations in Africa, could be procured here! . . . . . We have had since another meeting, when a society was organised for the Evangelisation of Africa, by means of native agency. The object has excited the deepest interest in the black population, and I have no doubt be shall we able to make a commencement at least. Your plan is much more extensive. I think you may rely on securing from the West Indies an agency of negro and coloured persons, efficient for establishments either civil or commercial, as might be thought advisable A good *common* education is generally within the reach of all classes now. . . . . . The negro is naturally a very susceptible creature, perhaps naturally the most favourably disposed of any of the human family, to receive and avail himself of the advantages which may be put in his way; but by some fatality, unaccountable on any principle, save that ' the time to favour it had not come,' the tribe has remained an outcast, and the country a waste.

" One poor African, named James Keats, left this country a few months ago, really on a pilgrimage to his native land, that he might carry the gospel there. We are anxious to hear of him. He had reached Sierra Leone, and had, I believe, embarked in Her Majesty's ship Rattlesnake for the Congo river, which he intends to ascend."

I have also received a letter from the Rev. John Beecham, stating that a number of agents might be obtained from among the Wesleyan negroes in the West Indies, who are already qualified for the work " to a good extent," and who, by the necessary training, might prove valuable auxiliaries to the cause.

The Rev. Mr. Holberton, Rector of St. John's, has also stated his views on the subject, in a letter to the Rev. Mr. Trew, dated Antigua, March 6, 1839, of which the following is an extract :—

" The subject of your circular has long occupied my mind; and now that it has come, soliciting inquiry on the point, I cannot help laying before you what seems to me a very feasible, and comparatively inexpensive mode of proceeding in this deeply in-

teresting work. Instead of having a college erected
in one of the islands for the reception of native black
and coloured youths of promise, I would respectfully
recommend that an agent be sent to *this* island, and
there gather about him a band of black and coloured
youths, to be trained and educated expressly for the
employments proposed in your letter, more especially
as missionaries. *Nothing is better than an infant
school as the first training place for the future
missionary*, as he is there likely to be moulded into
a pains-taking, persevering, simple-minded man.

" From persons so employed and approved, your
agent might make a selection. Such as he made
choice of should be trained by him, and domesticated
with him for a time; and when the necessary
measure of fitness was apparent, should be sent for
one year to the Church Missionary Society's college
in England. And when you forward them from
England, send as their superintendent, one of ourselves, a minister who shall direct their energies
aright, bear with their weaknesses, and keep united
heart and mind in the great work on which they had
been sent out. I do not see how you can move a
step in this great undertaking without sending out
an agent of decided piety, sound judgment, and competent ability, to instruct and direct those who are to
be committed to his charge; but let him be *no
sectarian*.

" On the whole, then, you will see that I do not
hold the scheme which you state in your letter to be

at all a visionary one; but am sanguine enough to hope, that if you proceed on the plan I have ventured to recommend, you will attain to the desired end by a very speedy, and sure and safe way. I rejoice in the prospect of such an undertaking. It will be the most righteous compensation that could be made to Africa for all the wrongs England, through former years, took part with other nations in doing to her. Of a truth how beautiful will be to her, the feet of the sons of those who were cruelly torn from her soil in years past, returning to her shores again with the everlasting gospel in their hands, and their mouths opened to declare unto her what God hath wrought."

The Rev. John Clark, baptist missionary in Jamaica, stated to me, in a letter dated September 16, 1839, " that the case of Africa was exciting deep sympathy amongst the members of his congregation." He also named several negroes, already qualified to some extent, who were willing and even anxious to enter immediately upon the work; and stated his full conviction that an ample number of native agents might, after suitable education, be available from the island of Jamaica, for the important purposes of African instruction.

ADVANCES ALREADY MADE.

To this it must be added that some advances have already been made. The Church Missionary Society have a normal school for the education of teachers

at Sierra Leone; by the last statement it appears
that sixteen are now in the course of education, under
the effective instruction of the Rev. G. A. Kissling,
who speaks favourably of his scholars. By a summary, issued May, 1839, it appears that there are
5098 of all ages under the care of this society; and
the report of this year states, " with thankfulness to
Almighty God, the steady progress of this first
established of the society's missions."

The Report of the Wesleyan mission for this year
has the following paragraph, p. 68 :—" The state of the
work at the West African stations is very gratifying,
and the openings for more extended usefulness are
most inviting. At Sierra Leone nearly 2000 persons are united together in religious fellowship, and
the schools are prosperous. The stations at the
Gambia are increasing in importance. At Macarthy's
island the committee for the civilisation department
are exerting themselves for the benefit of the converted natives. The kingdoms of Woolli and Bondou, which the enterprising spirit of Mr. Fox has
explored and other places, are open to the missionaries. At Cape Coast, the rapid spread of the
gospel calls for the most grateful acknowledgments
to Almighty God, who has crowned the labours
of his servants with signal success. And in the
midst of the discouragements resulting from the painful visitations of disease and death, which these missions from time to time experience, it is an alleviating
consideration that a native agency is rising up, by

which the work may at no distant period be prose-
cuted, without so large a sacrifice of life and health
on the part of European missionaries."

The Wesleyans have declared their intention to
establish a college on Macarthy's island for the education of children of natives of the higher classes, in
connexion with the experimental farm.   One benevolent individual, Dr. Lindoe, has engaged to give
£1000 to this institution.

The Church Missionaries have prepared, and with
the help of the Bible Society, printed, translations of
the gospel of St. Matthew in the Bullom, Mandingo,
and Susoo languages, in which they have also
printed grammars, or lesson-books, as well as .in the
Eyo or Aku,* and the Sherbro.   The American missionaries have published elementary books in the
Greybo and Bassa languages.   I have before mentioned the Wolof lessons of Hannah Kilham.   The
Rev. R. M. Macbrair, of the Wesleyan Society, has
published a complete grammar of the Mandingo.
Another Wesleyan missionary, the Rev. W. Arch-
bell, has published a grammar of the Sechuana language of South Africa, which has been also critically
investigated by the French missionary, M. Casalis,
and is supposed to be the key to the dialect prevailing
from the Congo to Delagoa bay.

---

* It is worthy of remark that the Aku language has been found
to be understood by the great majority of the captured negroes.
Mr. Ferguson is my authority for this: from this circumstance
important facilities are likely to arise.

I am not amongst the number of those who derive encouragement from the vicinity of the Mahomedans. I must confess that I apprehend a more stubborn resistance to the diffusion of knowledge, especially that which is the best and the most civilising, from the followers of the Prophet, than from the simple and docile, though barbarous, tribes of Central Africa. Mahomedanism also gives the sanction of religion to the Slave Trade, and even enjoins it as a mode of converting the heathen. That people are " Kaffering, and do not say their prayers, the dogs!" is sufficient reason for the true believers making war upon them,* and carrying them into slavery. Their prejudices are so deeply rooted, that some missionaries do not hesitate to say they would rather deal with Pagans than with Mahomedans.

Yet even with these there is some encouragement; to a certain extent they go along with us. There are points in the Mahomedan faith which we may turn to account in attempting to introduce better instruction. The Mussulmans of the west do not regard Christians with the same horror as those of the east; they seem to be favourably impressed by finding that we acknowledge much of their own sacred history ; and with them, the names of Abraham and Moses serve to recommend our holy books.

We may make common cause also with them in Africa, in our common abhorrence of the bloody rites and sacrifices of the Pagans. Thus Mr. Hutchison

* Denham, p. 149.

writes from Coomassie :—" This place now presents the singular spectacle of a Christian and a Mahomedan agreeing in two particulars—rejecting fetishes, and absenting themselves from human sacrifices and other abominations. The rest of the people, of whatever country they may be, when the king's horns announce anything of the kind, strive who will get there first, to enjoy the agonies of the victims !"

Hitherto education has been entirely in the hands of the Mahomedans ; and in fact, the Arabic is, to a considerable extent, the common language of Central Africa.

The travels of the Mahomedans have to a certain degree enlarged their minds. They are the leaders of most of the caravans, and some travel merely for pleasure. Mr. Fox mentions seeing at Macarthy's Island, a Moor who had come across the continent from Medina, and was much interested on being shown on a map the places he had passed through. " When questioned as to the object he had in view in coming so far, his answer was, he merely came for 'take walk'—' he wished to see the Gambia, Senegal, &c.'" Mr. Fox gave him the New Testament in Arabic, which he read with tolerable ease.

It becomes evident, therefore, that our way is not totally blocked up, but that there are many circumstances which will tend to facilitate our efforts for disseminating knowledge and religion among those who are the objects of our sympathy. And the encouragement and stimulus to exertion which we derive from these, ought to be in proportion to the

magnitude of the enterprise we contemplate, and of
the results we expect will follow. The elevation of
the native mind, as it is the only compensation
we can offer for the injuries we have inflicted on
Africa, so it is the truest, the cheapest, and the
shortest road to the downfall of the Slave Trade, and
of those frightful superstitions which it has tended to
preserve.

In what way, then, can this advance of mind be
most effectually and speedily attained?   I answer in
the words of Mr. Burke, when speaking on a kindred
subject,* " I confess I trust more, according to the
sound principles of those who have at any time
ameliorated the state of mankind, to the effect and influence of religion, than to all the rest of the regula-
tions put together." The Gospel ever has been, and
ever must be, the grand civiliser of mankind. Happily for Africa, a mass of evidence is to be found cor-
roborative of this assertion, in the Report of the Committee of the House of Commons in the sessions 1833
and 1834, on the Aborigines Question, appointed to
consider, amongst other things, " what measures
ought to be adopted to promote the spread of civilisation among the Aborigines of our colonies, and to lead
them to the peaceful and voluntary reception of the
Christian religion."   A main branch of that inquiry
was, " Whether the experience of the several missionary societies led to the belief that it would be
advisable to begin with civilisation in order to intro-

* Burke's Works, vol. ix. p. 287 : Letter to Dundas on Civilisation of Negroes in the Two Hemispheres.

duce Christianity, or with Christianity in order to lead to civilisation." It is a striking fact, that the representatives of the missionary bodies who were examined on that occasion, without any previous concert between themselves on the subject of the inquiry, arrived at precisely the same conclusion, namely, " That there is no means so effectual, under the divine blessing, to benefit man for ' the life that now is,' as well as ' that which is to come,' as Christianity."

In proof of this, Mr. Coates, secretary of the Church Missionary Society, observes to the committee :

" I find the preceptive part of Christianity tends to make man peaceable, honest, sober, iudustrious, and orderly. These, in my opinion, are the very elements of civilisation, in the moral sense of it.

" The impression of its great principles on the heart tends directly to make him humble, self-denying, philanthropic, beneficent, apart from the consideration of those effects which may be deemed more strictly of a religious or theological kind. I see in it, therefore, an arrangement and process by which the human mind is to be operated upon in a more powerful manner than by any other agency that can be imagined.

" If I look at the world when, at the rise of Christianity, it found Rome in the zenith of her power and glory, in the highest state of civilisation, as civilisation could exist in a heathen land, at that period, among other practices, that of selling their prisoners of war into slavery, prevailed. I find, too, in their gladiatorial games, man opposed to man in mortal conflict. And this not an accidental occurrence, or a scene exhibited in private, but habitually at their theatres, and to the most polished and distinguished of the whole population. What do I find at the expiration of a few ages? Christianity gains the ascendancy, and these things are extinct.

" I would only attempt further to illustrate this bearing of the subject from three or four facts of a recent date. At a recent period, suttees prevailed throughout our possessions in India—they are now prohibited: and this was effected by the expression of Christian opinion and feeling in this country. I look back on the enormous evils of the Slave Trade. The Slave Trade is suppressed, and suppressed unquestionably by the force of Christianity in this country. I come to a still more recent period, and see slavery abolished throughout all the British colonies, and that at the cost of £20,000,000 of public money; the result most unquestionably of the state of Christian principle and feeling.

" I now take up the question under a different aspect—I mean as it is illustrated by the effects of modern Protestant missions. I notice more particularly those of the Church Missionary Society.

" Mr. George Clarke, a catechist, who has been twelve years in New Zealand, thus writes:—' Here are a number of poor cannibals collected from the different tribes around us, whose fathers were so rude, so savage, that for ten years the first missionaries lived among them, often expecting to be devoured by them. A few years ago, they were ignorant of every principle of religion; had glutted in human blood, and gloried in it; but now there is not an individual among them who is not in some degree acquainted with the truths of the Christian religion. Not six years ago they commenced with the very rudiments of learning; now many of them can read and write their own language with propriety, and are completely masters of the first rules of arithmetic. But very few years ago a chisel made out of stone was their only tool; now they have not only got our tools, but are learning to use them.'

" Mr. R. Davis thus writes from the same mission: —' During the last quarter my time was principally occupied in preparing agricultural implements, and in attending to my natives employed about different work—carpentering, sowing, fencing, taking up the potato crop, and clearing land for the plough.'"

We next turn our attention to the testimony of another labourer in the Christian field, who no less strongly supports the preceding statements.

The Rev. John Beecham, of the Wesleyan Missionary Society, after expressing similar opinions to those delivered by Mr. Coates, as to the sole efficacy of Christianity in establishing and promoting refinement and civilisation, with their attendant comforts, and very clearly illustrating his idea by a reference to ancient history, proceeds further to support his sentiments by referring to the testimony of Kahkewaquonaby,* a chief of the Chippeway Indians, whose

* The literal meaning of Kahkewaquonaby is " Sacred," or

name has been subsequently changed into Peter Jones. This tribe, notwithstanding their rejection of the offers of Government made to induce them to renounce their roving course of life, afterwards embraced the gospel when preached to them, and devoted themselves to the pursuits of civilized life.

Mr. Jones thus writes:—" The improvements which the Christian Indians have made, have been the astonishment of all who knew them in their pagan state. The change for the better has not only extended to their hearts and feelings, but also to their personal appearance, and their domestic and social condition. About ten years ago this people had no houses, no fields, no horses, no cattle. Each person could carry upon his back all that he possessed, without being much burthened. They are now occupying about forty comfortable houses, most of which are built of hewn logs, and a few of frame, and are generally one and a half story high, and about twenty-four feet long and eighteen feet wide, with stone or brick chimneys ; two or three rooms in each house. Their furniture consists of tables, chairs, bedsteads, straw mattresses, a few feather beds, window curtains, boxes, and trunks for their wearing apparel, small shelves fastened against the wall for their books, closets for their cooking utensils, cupboards for their plates, knives and forks; some have clocks and watches.

" Eagle's feathers ;" the chief being of the Eagle tribe. He was baptised by the name of Peter, and assumed the name of Jones from his sponsor.

They have no carpets, but a few have mats laid on their floors. This tribe owns a saw-mill, a workshop, a blacksmith's shop, and a warehouse, the property of the whole community. They have about 200 acres of land under cultivation, on which they grow wheat, Indian corn, potatoes, &c. In their gardens they raise vegetables of various kinds, and a few have planted fruit trees. They have a number of oxen, cows, horses, and pigs; a few barns and stables; a few wagons and sleighs; and all sorts of farming implements.

" The gospel has of a truth now proved the ' savour of life unto life,' among our poor degraded women. The *men* now make the houses, plant the fields, provide the fuel and provisions for the house ; the business of the women is to manage the household affairs. The females eat with the men at the same table. You will be glad to hear that they are not insensible to the great things the gospel has done for them. I have often heard them expressing their thanks to the Great Spirit for sending them missionaries to tell them the words of eternal life, which have been the means of delivering them from a state of misery and degradation."

The testimony of the Rev. William Ellis, secretary of the London Missionary Society, is to the same effect. " True civilization and Christianity," he observes, " are inseparable ; the former has never been found but as a fruit of the latter." And he proceeds to show with much force and perspicuity, the inefficiency of a mere demi civilization to penetrate to the root of human evil, and to lead to comfort and to Christianity.

In the report of the London Missionary Society for 1835, a comprehensive view is taken of the effects produced by its labours in the South Sea Islands, and which may serve as an illustration of the benign and salutary influences of Christian truth, when perseveringly pressed upon the acceptance of the most barbarous people. The report observes,—" Forty years ago, when this society was formed, the islands of the South Seas had been discovered, explored, and abandoned, as presenting no objects worthy of further regard. Their inhabitants were sunk still lower in wretchedness by intercourse. with foreigners, and left a prey to the merciless idolatry that was fast sweeping them from the face of the earth. To them the attention of our venerable fathers in this cause was first directed, and a mission was auspiciously commenced. Idolatry was subverted, infant murder and human sacrifices ceased, education was promoted, converts flocked around the missionaries, churches were gathered, missionary societies formed, and teachers sent forth, Now, the people, fast rising in the scale of nations, have, as fruits of the Divine blessing on missionary perseverance, a written language, a free press, a representative government, courts of justice, written laws, useful arts, and improved resources. Commercial enterprise is promoting industry and wealth, and a measure of domestic comfort, unknown to their ancestors, now pervades their dwellings. A nation has been born at once, and surrounding nations have been blessed through their mercy."

Testimonies of this kind might be multiplied to a great extent. The annals of missionary proceedings teem with information of the most conclusive character, whilst the newly converted heathen themselves, ever ready to testify to the blessings they are thus brought to enjoy, are heard to exclaim, " But for our teachers, our grass on the hills, our fences and houses, would have been fire ashes long ago; and we should have been upon the mountains squeezing moss for a drop of water, eating raw roots, and smothering the cries of our children by filling their mouths with dirt, grass, or cloth." "We were all blind till the bird flew across the great expanse with the good seeds in its mouth, and planted them among us. We now gather the fruit, and have continual harvest."

No less striking is the evidence of Andrew Stoffell, a converted Hottentot, before the Aborigines Committee. He is asked, " Have the character and condition of the Hottentots been improved since the missionaries came among them, and in what respects?" He replies, "The young people can now read and write, and we all wear clothes; many of us have learned trades, and we are altogether better men. We have ploughing, wagon-makers, and shoemakers, and other tradesmen, amongst us. We can make all those things, except a watch and a coach. The missionaries have done much good, and they have tamed the Hottentots."

The testimony of Mr. Elisha Bates, who was a member of the Society of Friends, before the same Committee, furnishes the most convincing evidence of the efficacy of Christianity in promoting the improvement of the temporal condition of savage nations, even where other means had failed. He observes, speaking of the Indians of the United States, "Within the last few years we have had occasion to review the whole course of our proceedings, and we have come to the conclusion, from a deliberate view of the past, that we erred in the plan which was originally adopted, in making civilization the first object ; for we cannot count on a single individual that we have brought to the full adoption of Christianity." Having been further asked, "Do your Society now regret that they did not begin with Christianity, in order to lead the way to other advantages ; and if you had to recommence the same undertaking, would you now begin with Christianity ?" he emphatically replied, "Decidedly we should, from a full conviction that the attempt to civilize without Christianity has failed ; and that the plan now adopted is to make Christian instruction the primary object."

From these facts, gathered from different sources, the inference does not appear by any means doubtful, that whatever methods may be attempted for ameliorating the condition of untutored man, THIS alone can penetrate to the root of the evil, can teach him to love and to befriend his neighbour, and cause him to act as a *candidate* for a higher and holier state of being.

The hope, therefore, of effecting Africa's civilization, and of inducing her tribes to relinquish the trade in man, is, without this assistance, utterly vain. This mighty lever, when properly applied, can alone overturn the iniquitous systems which prevail throughout that continent. Let missionaries and schoolmasters, the plough and the spade, go together, and agriculture will flourish; the avenues to legitimate commerce will be opened; confidence between man and man will be inspired; whilst civilization will advance as the natural effect, and Christianity operate as the proximate cause of this happy change.

If, indeed, it be true that such effects will follow in the train of religion, and that Christianity alone can effect such changes and produce such blessings, then must we pause before we take a single step without it. The cause of Africa involves interests far too great, and results far too stupendous to be trifled with. The destinies of unborn millions, as well as of the millions who now exist, are at stake in the project; and the question is one of life or of death, of comfort and happiness, or of unutterable misery.

I believe that Christianity will meet the necessities of the case, and will prove a specific remedy for the moral evils of Africa.

My next proposition consequently is, that it is our duty to apply this remedy if we can.

One part of our national debt to Africa has already been acknowledged by the emancipation of our colonial slaves. There remains yet, however, a larger debt uncancelled,—that of restitution to Africa itself. We shall have much difficulty in ascertaining the amount of this obligation. Had we the means of discovering the total number of the sufferers whose miseries we have caused, or could we form the faintest idea of the nature and extent of the woes which are justly chargeable upon us as a nation, the duty of making reparation to Africa would be obvious.

Next to the debt which we ourselves owe, I can form no conception of a stronger argument in favour of carrying thither civilization and Christianity, than the existence of the Slave Trade itself, as it is found at this day, attended, on the one hand, by desolation; on the other, by a blind and devouring superstition; and in all directions encircled by ferocity and carnage, by torture, by terror, by all the evils through which man can be afflicted; and this variety of woes ending in the annual sacrifice of 500,000 human beings.

I repeat, that a stronger proof we cannot have, that it is the duty of the people of this empire to take up the cause upon Christian grounds, as a measure of atonement for the injuries we have done to her, as the only means now within our power of making restitution to her still degraded population; and as the most successful implement for uprooting from its very foundations that gigantic and accursed tree, which for ages has nourished beneath its shadow lamentation, and mourning, and woe.

Let but the people of this Christian country take up this cause *as a duty,* nationally and religiously, and no difficulties, however great, can, with the Divine blessing, hinder its success.

Nationally and religiously, the duty is plain. We have been put in trust with Christianity,—we have been the depositaries of a pure and holy faith, which inculcates the most expanded benevolence, and yet have not only neglected, as a nation, to confer upon Africa any real benefit, but have inflicted upon it a positive evil. Covetousness has dimmed our moral perceptions of duty, and paralysed our efforts, during many generations; and now that the nation has awakened from its lethargy, it is high time to act up to the principles of our religion.

Africa still lies in her blood. She wants our missionaries, our schoolmasters, our bibles, all the machinery we possess, for ameliorating her wretched condition. Shall we, with a remedy that may safely be applied, neglect to heal her wounds? Shall we, on whom the lamp of life shines, refuse to disperse her darkness?

" If there be any consolation in Christ, if any comfort of love, if any fellowship of the spirit, if any bowels of mercies,"* we must awake to the duty, amidst every difficulty, of freely and liberally distri-

* 1 Cor. vi. 9.

buting to others those rich and abundant blessings which have been entrusted to us.

I dwell no longer on the point of duty, but proceed to prove that *we can* apply the remedy.

I have dwelt the longer on the facilities which exist for the instruction of the natives, in order to show that the attempt to raise negro intellect, and to impart moral culture and religious instruction, is not of that forlorn character which many suppose. The facts I have stated are, I apprehend, sufficient to show that there is, amongst the Africans, a capability of receiving instruction; that there are agents within our reach, well calculated to assist in conferring it; that there is, in many parts at least, a thirst for education, and a readiness to accept the services of missionaries; and that, although the steps already taken have been very few, there has been some little advance. Other circumstances render the project of sending instructors more feasible at the present than at any former time. They will be carried to their destination by water. British steamers will be upon the Niger to protect them (at the only time that missionaries want protection) on their first settlement among the natives. Missionaries find less difficulty than any other class of persons, perhaps, in winning the confidence of native tribes. The secret of their success, is, the spirit of fair dealing, and the manifestation of upright and benevolent intentions, which they carry with them. These speak to all men, but especially to the uncivilised, in a language which they accurately comprehend, and to which they freely respond. It would seem, then, that the difficulties, considered a few years ago insurmountable, in the way of an attempt to diffuse intellectual, moral, and religious knowledge amongst millions of the human race, plunged in the very depths of ignorant superstition, have been in a great measure removed. Hence it is evident, that the question is not so much as to our power, but as to our willingness, to provide the means of conferring the inestimable benefits of intellectual advancement and true religion.

Having arrived at this point, it will naturally be asked, what scheme of instruction do I propose? I answer, I hardly dare to propose any scheme. Would that there were that charity among the Christians of the happier quarters of the world, which would induce them to lay aside their minor differences, in order to make a combined effort, of the most determined and strenuous character, to pour instruction upon Africa! But if this unity be too much and too good to be expected, we may at least hope that every department of the Christian church will separately press forward into that vast field which will, I trust, speedily be opened, and where there is room enough and need enough, physically and morally, for all.*

* I have no fear that missionaries to Africa will be wanting from our own country; but it gives me satisfaction to find the following passage in the South African Commercial Advertiser:—
" It will be agreeable to all who can comprehend the grandeur of

I may, however, recommend—

Firstly. That in every settlement formed on the views here laid down, the religious, moral, and industrial education of the natives should be considered an essential and fundamental object, claiming the early and careful attention of the founders of such settlement,

Secondly. That missionary societies should, by mutual agreement, subdivide and apportion the parts of this common field, so that each section of the Christian church may have undisturbed possession of its own sphere of labour.

Thirdly. That immediate arrangements should be made by each for normal schools,* intended to rear

this opening prospect, to learn that the people of the United States of America have determined to unite with the discoverers and regenerators of Africa. In a private letter, addressed to a gentleman of this colony, which we have just seen, the writer, one of the heads of a college in New Jersey, announces the deep interest which this subject has already excited in that country; and he inquires, with an anxiety approaching to impatience, as to the course their first missionaries should take, and the regions in which they are likely to be most useful. Thirty students in that college, he says, will be ready to start in a few months. At present their views are chiefly directed to Central Africa. It is not improbable, therefore, that they may follow the course of the newly-opened Niger."

* I am happy to say that this suggestion is by no means a novel one. In 1835, the Moravians contemplated a plan for establishing an institution in Jamaica, " for training native missionaries and teachers for needy Africa." The Rev. Hugh Stowell has recently proposed " an institution akin to Bishop's College, in the East

not only native teachers of religion, but native artizans, mechanics, and agriculturists, well instructed for the purpose, and themselves converts to Christianity.

Fourthly. That the African Civilization Society now being instituted shall befriend and protect all who are engaged in disseminating the truths of Christianity.

My object will be attained if two things are effected,—if a spirit of harmony shall reign amongst all who devote themselves to the benefit of Africa,— and if, wherever channels of commerce are opened, or agricultural locations made, there shall be put in operation at the same moment a system of instruction which shall raise up and send forth teachers of all that Africa requires to learn.

Indies, where those of the liberated Africans and of their teeming offspring who should give promise of distinguished piety and talent might be educated as future missionaries to the land of their forefathers." He goes on to say that, " without the services of converted natives, humanly speaking, very extended success cannot be anticipated. If, in other countries, this principle holds good, how much more in the case of Africa. There the fatality of the climate to European constitutions, the untamed savageness of the interior tribes, and the multiplicity of their motley dialects, present next to insuperable barriers to other than aboriginal agency."

CHAPTER VII.

SPECIFIC STEPS TO BE TAKEN.

I HAVE sufficiently explained what my object is. *It is the deliverance of Africa, by calling forth her own resources.* We contemplate that her population, instead of being sold into Foreign Slavery, and of perishing by tens of thousands in the process of transportation, shall be employed in the tillage, and in the commerce, which may be found at home.

In order to do this, we must

    1st. Impede and discourage the Slave Traffic.

    2ndly. Establish and encourage legitimate commerce.

    3rdly. Promote and teach agriculture.

    4thly. Impart moral and religious instruction.

To accomplish the *first*, we must

    Increase and concentrate our squadron, and make treaties with the chiefs of the coast, the rivers, and the interior.

To accomplish the *second*, we must

    Obtain commanding positions; settle factories; and send out trading-ships.

To accomplish the *third*, we must

    Set on foot an agricultural company.

    Obtain, by treaty, lands for cultivation, with so much power as may be necessary to keep the slave-trader at a distance.

The territory we obtain should be freely offered to us, without any kind of constraint.

It should be in the vicinity of some navigable river.

The climate should be, for Africa, healthy.

The soil should be capable of growing tropical productions.

Its limits should be extensive.

To accomplish the *fourth*, we must

Support the benevolent association now established.

Besides these special purposes, there is one general object, which must be carefully provided for, viz. : that the agents employed in Africa, whether on their own account, or in connection with an association at home ; whether engaged in commerce, cultivation, or instruction, may be *sufficiently protected*.

———————

Of the work to be done, a part belongs to the Government, and a part must be executed by individuals.

The Government should

Take on itself the whole duty and expense of preserving the peace, and of affording the necessary protection, to new British settlements in Africa.

Increase and concentrate our naval force.

Obtain Fernando Po, and such other commanding positions as may be found necessary.

Prepare, — instruct, — and send out embassies, with all practicable dispatch, (or authorize their African governors,) to form treaties, including either, or all, of the following points, viz. :—Prevention of Slave-traffic ;—arrangements for legitimate trade or cultivation,—with such privileges and powers as may be necessary for their well-doing ; and with grants of land for cultivation.

The part which devolves on individuals interested in the fate of Africa is,—

1st. Strenuously to assist the benevolent association already mentioned, the objects of which are—to assist individuals or societies who may engage themselves in the task of educating the population of Africa ;—to promote by every means in its power,—direct and indirect,—its civilization, cultivation, and commerce ; to obtain and circulate statistical, geographical, and all other information concerning that country, especially availing itself of the opportunity shortly to be presented of doing so, by appointing agents to accompany the expedition, which it is intended to send out in the ensuing autumn; and, lastly, to keep alive the interest of the people of England on the subject.

2ndly. To form an agricultural company, which shall, hereafter, send out persons well acquainted with tropical climates and produc-

tions; to form settlements, guided by such
arrangements and treaties as the Government
may have made; to commence pattern farms
and establish factories, well supplied with European goods; in a word, to use all the means
that experience may point out, for a profitable and successful employment of British
skill and capital in the African continent. *No
Slavery, no monopoly, forbearance towards
the natives, and utter enmity towards Slave
Trade and Slavery in all their forms,* must
be the fundamental principles of such a company; and an honest adherence to these will,
in my full belief, insure its prosperity and profit.

I have proposed two associations, a Benevolent
Society, which shall watch over and befriend the interests of Africa, and a Company, which shall cultivate her soil. In one sense they are entirely separate; the object of the one is, charity,—of the other,
gain. As they are distinct in their principle, so, I
think, they ought to be kept entirely separate in the
prosecution of their details. Yet, it is impossible
that they should not subserve and benefit each other.
It is impossible to spread education, scientific knowledge, and the civilizing influence of Christianity,
without communicating that to the population, which
will most materially contribute to the advance of
commerce and agriculture: on the other hand, there
is no better way of advancing the moral and physical
condition of the people, than by the introduction of

our skill, and the sagacious and successful employment of our capital amongst them.*

To the question which has already been repeatedly
put to me, by those who have been moved to compassion by the sorrows of Africa, *What shall we do?*
my answer is,—Join the African Institution, which
we are endeavouring to revive; and join the African
Agricultural Association, which we are about to establish.

* Statements and proposals of a more definite nature respecting these two associations will, I trust, be laid before the public at
no distant day. In the mean time, it may be well to observe, in
answer to the inquiry in what manner it is proposed to work land
in Africa, that it is intended that those employed as superintend-
ents should be, as far as possible, of negro-extraction, but that
none should be sent but men of moral and religious character.
That such are to be had I have, I trust, shown in the Chapter on
the Elevation of Native Mind (page 491).

But in what species of agriculture is it proposed to employ
them? In the first instance, perhaps, in the cultivation of cotton;
on the facilities for which I have dwelt at some length (page 332);
but as we become better acquainted with Africa, we shall know
how to turn its cultivation to the best advantage, and of course we
shall grow those articles which will find the readiest and most
profitable market in the civilized world.

CONCLUSION.

I CANNOT close this work, without suggesting some considerations, which, in the review I have taken of the whole subject, have forcibly impressed themselves on my own mind. Great as is the undertaking, there are, at the present time, many concurrent and favourable circumstances, which have not previously existed.

England is at peace. Since the abolition of the Slave Trade by Great Britain, it is not too much to say, that there has been, both at home and amongst many of the nations of the continent, an increase of a benevolent and enlightened spirit. Our sincerity with regard to the Slave Trade has been established, by sacrifices which admit of no misconstruction. The principles involved in that great measure have been carried out by the abolition of slavery, and by the willingness of the nation to pay the price of that most costly act of duty. Thus, then, we are in a condition (our own hands being clean) to ask the co-operation of France, Russia, the United States, and other great powers; and we have a right to demand from Spain, Portugal, and Brazil that they should no longer delay the execution of their engagements.

Again, there are certain circumstances, which render Africa far more accessible than at any former

R

period. We now know the course of the Niger,
and an entrance into the centre of Africa is opened,
by means of this noble river. We have now got, in
steam, a power which enables us to traverse it; to
pass rapidly through the unhealthy parts of it;
to ascend it against the current; in short, to command its navigation.

Beyond, and besides all these, there is another
circumstance lately brought into existence which
may supply us with the necessary agents capable of
enduring the African climate. I wish not, with too
sanguine an eye, to anticipate the course of events,
but I cannot help believing, as I have elsewhere
stated, that in the present condition of the negro
race in our West Indian colonies lies one of the
best hopes of Africa. They are rising, under the
influence of freedom, education, and religion, to a
rank, which will fit them to be messengers of peace
to the land from which their fathers were torn; and
already, though the time has been so short, various,
distinct, and unconcerted symptoms have appeared,
proving that " it pitieth them to see her in the dust."

At the moment, then, that a highway is discovered
into the heart of Africa, and that a new power is
placed in our hands enabling us to command its
navigation, and that agents present themselves qualified by physical constitution to endure the climate,
and by intellectual cultivation to carry with them
the seeds of true improvement; at that moment, we
learn the utter fallacy and inutility of the system for

the suppression of the Slave Trade which we have hitherto been pursuing.

But there is another consideration, though quite of a different order, which bears strongly upon this point. New markets for the sale of our manufactured articles are urgently required, at a time when we are excluded from some of our accustomed channels of sale.

Nor is the supply of the raw material less important; new fields for its growth ought to be opened, in proportion to the increasing consumption of the world. I firmly believe that, if commercial countries consulted only their true interests, without reference to motives of a higher character, they would make the most resolute and persevering attempts to raise up Africa—not to divide her broad territory amongst them, nor to enslave her people, but in order to elevate her into something like an equality with themselves, for their reciprocal benefit.

But I am well aware that it is a case in which we must act under circumstances of considerable discouragement; and especially that of our great ignorance with regard to the real internal condition of Africa, both physical and moral.

Upon any other subject, the dimness of our knowledge would supply an unanswerable reason for pausing; but the state of Africa admits no delay. The complicated horrors which are crowded into the space of a single month, furnish sufficient reasons for all possible dispatch, and for adventuring on measures, which, under other circumstances, would be premature and probably rash.   Better to fall into a thousand errors in the detail, and to incur the expense and mortification of the miscarriages they will cause, than to sit still, and leave Africa to her woeful fate.

If nothing be done, Africa will be at the end of 50 or 100 years what she now is, and we shall still be as ill-informed, as we now are, of the readiest means for her relief.   But if we grapple with the evil, we shall either find ourselves in the right road, or grope our way to it; and the very mistakes we now make will serve to direct us aright hereafter.

I am not so sanguine as to suppose that we can at once, by a single effort, solve the problem which lies before us.   The deliverance of Africa will put our patience and perseverance to no ordinary trial. We must deliberately make up our minds to large and long-continued expense, to persevering labours, and to severe disappointments.   I wish not in any degree to conceal from myself, or from others, these truths.

But the question is,—Shall such an experiment be made ?   There are two mighty arguments which should prompt us to such an undertaking: the intense miseries of Africa, and the peculiar blessings which have been showered upon this country by the mercy of Divine Providence.   With regard to the first, I need not again plunge into the sickening details of the horrors which accompany this bloody trade, and of the sanguinary rites, which there bear the name of religion. Whether we look to the vast space which is there made a theatre of public misery, or calculate how many deeds of cruelty and carnage must be perpetrated every day in the year, in order to make up the surprising total of human distress, which, by indisputable documents, we know to be realized, there is enough to awaken the deepest pity, and to arouse the most energetic resolution.

Turning to the second consideration, we cannot fail to see how signally this nation has been preserved, and led forward to an extent of power and prosperity, beyond what almost any other nation has been permitted to reach. "It is not to be doubted that this country has been invested with wealth and power, with arts and knowledge, with the sway of distant lands, and the mastery of the restless waters, for some great and important purpose in the government of the world. Can we suppose otherwise than that it is our office to carry civilization and humanity, peace and good government, and, above all, the knowledge of the true God, to the uttermost end of the earth?" *

Since that passage was written, Great Britain has refuted the idle, yet once the all but universal doctrine, that confusion, havoc, and bloodshed must follow the extinction of slavery. And with this doctrine of universal convulsion has also fallen the

---

* The Rev. Mr. Whewell's Sermon before the Trinity Board.

allegation, that negroes will not work, except under the impulse of the whip. It is confessed by every authority, that wages have charmed away what used to be called " the natural and incurable indolence of the African." I do not say a single word here upon the controverted question, whether the negroes demand excessive remuneration. We may assume, for the sake of argument, that they are exorbitant. This may be a fault, though, under all the circumstances, not an unnatural or surprising one ; but this does not touch my assertion, grounded upon all the papers which have been produced to Parliament, that, when satisfied with the rate of wages, they do labour industriously, and execute more work, in better style, and in less time, than when they were slaves. There never was a greater delusion, than that negroes could not be induced to work for money.

A nobler achievement now invites us. I believe that Great Britain can, if she will, under the favour of the Almighty, confer a blessing on the human race. It may be that at her bidding a thousand nations now steeped in wretchedness, in brutal ignorance, in devouring superstition, possessing but the one trade, and that one the foulest evil that ever blighted public prosperity, or poisoned domestic peace, shall, under British tuition, emerge from their debasement, enjoy a long line of blessings—education, agriculture, commerce, peace, industry, and the wealth that springs from it; and, far above all, shall willingly receive that religion which, while it confers innumerable temporal blessings, opens the way to an eternal futurity of happiness.

I have already confessed that I am not experienced or skilful in matters which touch the commercial part of the question. I tread this ground with diffidence. I say no more, than that it appears to me that the soil in Africa being rich, and the people being found upon it, it is not advisable to carry them to a distance. It is possible, however, that some fallacy, unsuspected by me, may lurk under my theory, if theory of mine it can be called; but when I come to humanity, justice, and the duties of Christian men, I stand upon a rock. It may be, or it may not, that while we act under the impulse of charity to the most afflicted of mankind, we are also obeying the dictates of the most far-sighted policy, and the most refined ambition. It may prove, or it may not, that while we are leading Africa to grow at home, cheaper sugar than Brazil, and cheaper cotton than the United States, we are renovating the very sinews of our national strength. Be this as it may, without doubt it is the duty of Great Britain to employ the influence and the strength which God has given her, in raising Africa from the dust, and enabling her, out of her own resources, to beat down Slavery and the Slave Trade.

I am aware that it is quite a different question whether the means I propose are practicable, and likely to be crowned with success. It belongs to the nation to consider whether the suggestions now

offered, and the policy which I have ventured to recommend, are likely to eradicate that mighty evil
which desolates Africa, degrades Europe, and afflicts
humanity. If it shall appear that my views are not
chimerical,—that they have some grounds of reason in
themselves, and are fortified by a great mass of evidence of a practical nature,—and if it shall appear
that, whether we look to the great interests of humanity, or consult the prosperity and honour of the British empire, it is our duty to proceed, undeterred by
difficulty, peril, or expense,—then I trust that steps
will be taken boldly and rapidly, for the accomplishment of the object.

But if it shall appear that this, and every other
plan is likely to be futile, or, if the Government shall
not feel itself justified in braving the difficulties and
expense which will be required, then must I express
my painful conviction, that it would be better for the
interests of humanity that we should withdraw altogether from the struggle;—better to let the planters
of America satiate themselves with their victims,
than to interpose our efforts, unavailing in reducing
the magnitude of the evil, while they exasperate the
miseries which belong to it,—better to do nothing than
to go on, year after year, at great cost, adding to the
disasters, and inflaming the wounds of Africa. But I
cannot contemplate such a result,—I must hope better
things.

The case is now fairly laid before the nation. It
belongs to no individual, to no party,—it is a distinct

and isolated question. My desire has been to lay it upon the national conscience of Great Britain. There I must leave it; having fully stated what I believe to be the only remedy, and the best means of applying that remedy.

I find, in the sacred writings, a faithful picture of sorrows,—such as those with which Africa is now afflicted; but I find also annexed to that description a prophetic promise, which we must fervently desire to see realised to miserable Africa:—

" Thus saith the Lord of Hosts,—Before these days there was no hire for man, nor any hire for beast: neither was there any peace to him that went out, or came in, because of the affliction : for I set all men, every one against his neighbour.

" But now I will not be unto the residue of this people as in the former days, saith the Lord of Hosts.

" For the seed shall be prosperous ; the vine shall give her fruit, and the ground shall give her increase, and the Heavens shall give their dews: and I will cause the remnant of this people to possess all these things."

APPENDIX A.

On Facilities of making Treaties.

THE following instances may prove the disposition of the native chiefs to form connexions with us :—

Sir Charles MacCarthy, in giving an account of the negotiations for taking possession of the Isles de Loss, states, that the treaty " was made with great facility, without drunkenness or bribery *." In 1826 the king of Barra ceded to Great Britain, by treaty, a tract of land on the northern shore of the Gambia, 36 miles in length, by one in breadth, for 400 Spanish dollars yearly; all slave-trading to be finally prohibited. In 1827 the king of Combo guaranteed to the British crown rights nearly amounting to sovereignty over his dominions, extending about 30 miles along the southern bank of the river, and 10 miles along the coast, and from 10 to 15 miles in breadth, with the prohibition of the Slave Trade, for an annual payment of 100 dollars.

Treaties with the king of Bulola and Biafra, made by Sir Neil Campbell, cede the sovereignty of those districts, and a right on the part of Great Britain to establish forts or factories, with clauses for the abolition of the Slave Trade. From the Pongas and Nunez rivers, little or no produce,

---

* Mr. Hutton, acting governor at the Gambia, effected an arrangement with the chief of Contalacunda, which being deemed a place of importance by our merchants, he did not consider 50 dollars annually (about 10*l.*) ill bestowed in securing its chief's friendship.

except slaves, is exported. In 1827, Sir N. Campbell saw the chiefs of these rivers, and obtained " the cession of the most commanding points up the mouth of each." Mr. Hutton states, in 1829, that he made a treaty with the king of Woolli at Fattatenda, and obtained the full sovereignty of that town, with stipulations in favour of our commerce, for the payment in merchandise of 200 dollars annually. He also made a treaty with the king of Bondou, and observes, " The object of 300 or 400 dollars is trifling, compared with the advantage that would result from such a connexion with both these kings, whose influence extends not only through the whole of Bondou and Woolli, but also to the adjoining countries of Shendrum and Tanda, celebrated for gold, gum, &c." Though we have not availed ourselves of these openings,—though the payments to the chiefs were soon suspended,—some benefit seems to have been derived from these engagements. Rev. T. W. Fox, a Wesleyan missionary, as appears from his journal in my possession, paid a visit to Woolli in 1837, and urged upon the king the benefits of Christianity : " He," says Mr. Fox, " listened attentively, appeared pleased, and said that was what he wanted; and if I would come and sit down on his ground, he would give me as much land as I wished, and his own children to be educated." I replied, " That if I sent a missionary, I hoped he would protect him, and not allow anybody to trouble him;" Koy (the king) answered, " that he *belonged* to white man, and that if *Tobaba fodey* (the white priest) came to sit down in his kingdom, nobody should, or would, trouble him." He also said, " he hoped God would preserve me; the object I had in view was very good."

The king of Bondou, also, whom Mr. Fox likewise visited in 1838, offered to give him ground for a settlement, and said, "They were all glad to see him, and they loved him

very much, because he was a good man." It is something
in the present disastrous condition of Africa, that there is
a good feeling towards the British, and no rooted indisposi-
tion to listen to their agents.

In 1827, the king and head men of Brekama solicited
Sir N. Campbell to take them under British protection:
they stipulated to renounce the Slave Trade, and to enter
into no wars, in return for British alliance, "and four pieces
of baft annually."

Governor Rendall gives a list of 19 kings or chiefs, on
the northern and 20 on the southern, bank of the Gambia,
with whom we have some intercourse or connexion. The
total sum annually divided amongst these, for rents and pro-
pitiatory presents, reaches only 300l. This liberality is
not without its effect. Governor Rendall reports 75l. spent
in presents to chiefs and head men, on both banks of the
river, between Bathurst and Woolli, and says, " This expenditure has not been in vain, as I have received intelligence that the war in Carbo, which has lasted 12 years, is
finally settled, both parties having taken my advice, and
called in umpires to decide their difference: the paths
through Carbo and Footah-Jallow will now be open to the
river, by which a great influx of trade must take place."
Besides the tribes lying immediately on the Gambia, Governor Rendall says, that " messengers are often received at
Bathurst from the kings of Boaul and Cayor, to the northward of Bondou; Cassan, and Kaarta-Bambarra, to the
eastward; and the Almanez of Footah-Jallow, to the south-
east." I am aware that no definite ideas can be derived
from this catalogue of barbarous chiefs: we have, however,
evidence sufficient to show that the soil is fertile, and suited
to tropical productions; that the forests are full of mahogany and valuable woods, and that the country yields gold:
hence we may justly infer, that from a territory so extensive,

for which nature has done so much, there is a capability of large cultivation, and of considerable commerce. The Commissioners of Inquiry sent out to that country in 1827, report thus,—" When the magnitude of the river Gambia, and the various countries through which it takes its course are duly considered, it will probably be concluded that, with capital and enterprise, its trade may be increased to a considerable extent ;" they add, and I entirely unite with them in the opinion, " Great as the advantages, in this point of view, which it presents, they can never be completely available, without the establishment of a more intimate and friendly intercourse with the natives of the country." Following the coast, we come to the Portuguese settlements of Cacheo and Bissao; and then to a belt of Slave-dealing states, extending to the Congo, and blocking out legitimate commerce from the interior. Here, however, we have some claims, of which we have not availed ourselves. The fine little island of Bulama, in the estuary of the Rio Grande, belongs to Great Britain : it is unoccupied ; and, in 1826, Governor Macaulay recommended that liberated Africans should be located there. I find, in Captain Beaver's " African Memoranda," the following report of the cession of this island to us :—" The original purchase of the island of Bulama, made by Captain Beaver in 1792, was effected without any difficulty; though, on the first arrival of the English, they had offended the natives by cutting wood without permission, and in the quarrel which ensued, some lives had been lost." When Captain Beaver entered into a palaver with the two kings of Canabac, touching the purchase of their hunting island of Bulama, one of them, while he attributed the affray to our taking the liberty to help ourselves, without any leave from the native authorities, expressed his desire to treat with us amicably on fair terms. He said, " He was sorry for what had happened, but that then they neither knew who we were, nor what were our intentions : we were strangers, and we took their land." Being, however, convinced of the pacific and just dispositions of the English, and of the great reciprocal benefits that were likely to result from an European colony established in their neighbourhood, they readily made over the sovereignty and possession of the said island to the king of Great Britain, for 473 bars of goods (about 78l. 16s. 8d.)

Two chiefs on the mainland afterwards put in a claim for a part of the price ; and Captain Beaver, having ascertained that "there was some justice in these people's claims," wisely satisfied them, and bought their concurrence in the cession of the island, together with a still larger tract on the mainland, for goods, the cost price of which he estimated at 25l. 13s. 1d. There were some further charges for European agency in these transactions.*

Captain Beaver, at all events, did not apprehend that there was any difficulty in his time in obtaining any extent of territory on reasonable terms : for he proposes to the Government, that they should purchase between the Gambia and the Rio Grande a tract of 18,000,000 of acres, which, in his opinion, might be bought for 5000l., or less.

* See the copy of these treaties in Johansen's "Account of Bulama and the Bulam Association," pp. 28, 29.

255

APPENDIX B.

Vide Page 34.

Abstract of a Letter written in 1835, relative to Fernando Po.

This island belongs to Spain, and was formerly called " Formosa," or the beautiful island, a designation it well deserves. It has three ranges of hills running parallel with the north-east side of it, the centre one rising into a mountain of about 10,000 feet in height. After some negotiation between the governments of England and Spain, it was agreed in 1827, that the former might place an establishment on the island for the purpose of locating upon it such negroes as might be captured, and emancipated, under the Slave Trade Abolition Treaties, and a governor was sent from hence, and various buildings were erected; but some difficulties arising, in consequence of the Spanish Crown refusing to transfer the sovereignty of the island, it was abandoned, after the outlay of a considerable sum. This termination of the negotiation is most deeply to be lamented, as the island, in the hands of Great Britain, would prove a most important and valuable possession as regards her commerce; but it would be still more important to the civilization of Africa, forming, as it does, the key to the centre of that vast continent, and in this view, to the philanthropist, its occupation by the British Crown would be invaluable, as the prepossession of the natives on the opposite coast (from which it is distant only a few miles) in favour of the English, over all other nations, is very remarkable : but to any maritime trading nation, it would prove a valuable acquisition.   The Americans have already shown a desire for opening a trade with it, and in 1834 one or two vessels were engaged in whaling there.

On the northern end of the island there is a very fine bay, where the different points of land form an inner and outer anchorage, and where from 400 to 500 vessels might ride in all the months of the year in complete security. The facilities for discharging and taking on board their cargoes are also very great, as they may lie in three or four fathoms of water within 40 or 50 feet of the shore, the depth increasing greatly at every additional few feet : it is remarkable, too, that these seas are not visited by the hurricanes so prevalent on other parts of the coast, and that even the tornadoes are less violent than elsewhere.   These advantages, joined to its immediate vicinity to the great rivers which penetrate to the heart of Africa, render it unnecessary to say a word to enforce the desirableness of its becoming an English possession.   At the period when the island was abandoned a town had been laid out at the head of the bay, a considerable number of houses had been built, and a good drainage cut through each street.   The population, then amounting to about 700 persons, were in a flourishing condition, being constantly employed in cutting timber, building, and cultivation, and the town was bidding fair to become one of the most—perhaps the most—important on the coast.   The native population, in its immediate vicinity, was estimated at between 500 and 600 persons, whose ready submission to the English government gave every facility to the progressive improvement of the new colony : they looked up to the whites, and readily received instruction in the schools which were established, and they attended church with great regularity and decency on the Sundays—on which days they came into the town in great numbers.

The island produces, in rich abundance, palm-oil, cocoas,

plantains, and yams ; and it is covered with a vast variety
of trees, many of them of the most useful qualities : there
are whole forests of palms, and many different kinds of
trees which would be valuable for cabinet work ; but, in
a commercial point of view, the most important amongst
its timber trees, and in which it also abounds, is that which
is peculiarly adapted for ship-building, and which may be procured of almost all lengths.   Several ships, both belonging
to the government and to merchants, have been repaired
with it at the island, and many cargoes have been imported
into England, and used in the king's and merchants' yards.
The palm-tree is invaluable to the negroes, who use palm-
wine as a beverage. The soil is so rich, that no limits can be
assigned to its productiveness : it is capable of producing
almost every luxury in the vegetable world for the use of
man and beast.

   Much has been urged in favour of, and also against, the
climate of this island ; but when the timber, with which it
abounds, is felled,—and this, if the island were occupied by
the British, would be constantly progressing, as it is, as has
been already stated, of a very valuable kind,—there can
scarcely be a doubt that it would become, ere very long, the
Madeira of the western coast : as almost any degree of temperature may be obtained on the different ranges of its mountains ; and the vegetables of the temperate as well as of the
tropical climates, flourish in its soil, which is extremely fertile.
The water, too, is pure and abundant ; game is plentiful, and
its coasts swarm with fish.   It is a fact well established,
that, in plains in tropical climates where fever exists at a
temperature of from 80° to 90°, it is not found on the neighbouring mountains, where at noon the thermometer does not
range higher than from 70° to 75°.

Extract of a Letter from another Gentleman, dated Clarence, Fernando Po, May, 1835.

" We anticipate with much anxiety the (we trust not very far distant) period, when this establishment will be again resumed by our government: for, on investigation into the real state of the colony, it must necessarily take place, and then prejudices will surely give way, and truth prevail over the false representations, through which, one of the most beautiful and profitable spots in Africa has been so injudiciously abandoned.   Indeed, I can, in addition to its beauty and great utility to British trade in Western Africa, safely say, that, in point of salubrity, if not more so, it is at all events equal to any other British settlement on the coast.

" Since ——'s departure, we have drawn up our militia, and designated it ' The Clarence Militia Corps,' and I feel great pleasure in stating, that, considering the short period the men have been under arms, and their natural awkwardness at first, I should not be ashamed to welcome the Commander-in-chief with a captain's guard, whenever Admiral Campbell will deign to honour us with a visit.

" Our little town of Clarence has also undergone some alterations and improvements ; the town, which formerly laid scattered in the midst of a forest of plantains and bananas, has been brought in nearer to the cove, and properly laid out ; the streets are made broad, and cut each other at right angles, on either side of which are the houses and allotments, of equal dimensions : so, that in what street soever you may be, instead of the suffocating atmosphere that formerly assailed one, you now enjoy a cool and refreshing current of air, which must certainly be conducive to health, and justify our anticipating even healthy wet seasons.

" While we go on thus improving among ourselves, I do not despair of working a complete revolution in the manners and habits of the aborigines, who are rapidly becoming inhabitants among us, and are already beginning to adopt our customs; assume a more active and industrious character; and supply us with much greater quantities of palm-oil than formerly."

APPENDIX C.

Copy of a Despatch from General Turner to Earl Bathurst

Dated Sierra Leone, January 25th, 1826.

" It is found that, under this system of putting them (the liberated Africans) to easy and regular labour such as they have been used to, on their landing from slave-ships, they become very orderly good labourers; but in the cases where they have been located in the villages, and have received gratuitous maintenance, they can, with difficulty, be induced to give a day's labour for good wages.

" It would but lead to disappointment to imagine that a large mass of poor ignorant people, without capital, skill, or industry, could be brought to maintain themselves, and to raise articles of export, without the assistance of labour-wages. Could such a system succeed even in England, the poor rates might soon be abolished."

General Turner further says, that if men of colour who understand the cultivation of cotton and coffee, were brought from the West Indies, to superintend such plantations as would not fail under such facilities to be formed by capitalists, he is satisfied much would be done in a few years for the improvement of the country.*

* Parliamentary Papers, Sierra Leone, p. 7, Session 1830, No. 57.

Copy of a Despatch from Lieutenant-Colonel Denham,* General Superintendent of the Liberated African Department.

Dated Sierra Leone, May 21st, 1827.

" What this colony, or rather the liberated Africans, have felt the most want of is, instruction, capital, and example: with the very little they have had of either, conveyed in a manner likely to benefit them generally, it is to me, daily, an increasing subject of astonishment, that the liberated Africans settled here have done so much for themselves as they have.

" I have not observed any disinclination for voluntary labour: it appears to be a system perfectly understood and practised by the liberated Africans here; and strengthens with their strength, as they become more sensible of the sweets of labour, by enjoying the profits of it, and the comforts those profits enable them to purchase: indeed, to the many hundreds of liberated Africans that have been employed as labourers on the different Government works, as well as on the buildings erected by private individuals, during the last few years, may in some measure be attributed the comparatively small number of agricultural labourers in the villages.

" Labourers' wages have varied from 1*s.* to 6*d.* per day: yet has there never been a deficiency of liberated Africans, who were willing to labour for hire. On the Naval Stores, now erecting by contract on King Tom's Point, are nearly 200 liberated African labourers, who work well and steadily, at 20*s.* per month, one-half paid in money, and the remainder in goods taken from the stores of the merchants who have the contract.

" The period of labour also forms a longer portion of the day here than even in the South of Europe, where for se-

* The celebrated African traveller, and eventually Governor of Sierra Leone.

veral hours, when the sun has most power, a general cessa-
tion of labour, or indeed employment, takes place. Labourers in this colony work from six in the morning till five
in the afternoon, constantly, with the exception of the hour
from nine till ten, which they are allowed for breakfast.

" Husbandry and practical agriculture should be encouraged by every possible means ; but yet I am inclined to
think the kind of labour in which so many of the liberated
Africans have been and still are employed, has been upon
the whole beneficial to them : they must acquire intelligence,
habits of regularity, and steady labour, with much general
knowledge, by being employed with artificers, and watch-
ing the progress of the public buildings from the foundation
to the roof,—the roof, to the finished whole,—as in the case
of the extensive Barracks, and a very handsome building·
intended for the Naval stores, which are both nearly completed.

" They are already sensible of the rewards of industry,
by being in possession of the profits; and the advantage of
property is becoming daily an increased object of interest.

" An anxious desire to obtain and enjoy the luxuries of
life is apparent in every village, from the oldest settler to
the liberated African of yesterday. European articles of
dress are the first objects of their desire, and for the means
of acquiring these both sexes will cheerfully labour; and a
gradual improvement has taken place in their dwellings, as
they become possessed of the necessary means for that purpose. Of the practicability of introducing free labour
amongst the liberated Africans settled here, I have not the
slightest doubt, nor do I believe they would work half as
well in any other way, unless the greatest cruelty should be
exercised towards them.

" My opinion on this subject is formed from facts, collected
during an actual residence in each of the settlements of

liberated Africans, of from one to three weeks, and I shall merely state those facts, as I consider them better than any reasoning. The number of frame-houses with stone foundations, and also stone houses, has increased in all the villages, particularly the mountain ones of Gloucester and Regent. Three sold during the last three years at Wellington. There are seven stone houses nearly finished, all begun during the last two years. The owners of these habitations, which cost them from 100 to 200 dollars, have all acquired the means of so permanently establishing themselves, by *free labour* and industry : they were all, with the exception of a few discharged soldiers from the Fourth West India Regiment, landed from the ships here after capture, and merely given a lot of ground and rations for a time : they became masons, carpenters, coopers, smiths, and farmers.

" The markets at Freetown are supplied with fruit and vegetables, almost exclusively, by the mountain villages ; and from 80 to 100 men, women, boys, and girls, are to be seen daily on the hill leading to Gloucester town, with the produce of their farms and gardens. This is also entirely the reward of their own industry and perseverance, for not the least instruction on this important branch of labour have they ever received."*

Major Ricketts in a despatch, dated June 30th, 1829, speaking of the produce raised by the liberated Africans, says :—

" The value of these articles may be estimated by the well-known fact, that a labouring man can go into the market and purchase as much food for a penny-halfpenny as will suffice for two meals. Some of the persons supplying the market are known to travel from Waterloo and Hastings, the former being 22, and the latter 16 miles from Freetown, carrying their produce in baskets on their heads. This kind

* Papers relative to Sierra Leone, September, 1830, No. 57. p. 15—17.

of industry clearly manifests the desire the liberated Africans have to labour voluntarily, to enable them, by honest means, to become possessed of those luxuries, which they see their more wealthy brethren enjoying."*

APPENDIX D.

Playford Hall, 17th July, 1839.

MY DEAR FRIEND,

Having read your little book, bearing the name of " The Remedy," I congratulate you on having at last discovered a way, which if followed up in all its parts, would most certainly lead to the abolition of that execrable traffic called the Slave Trade.

Two of the measures which you hold forth to accomplish this object, are the employment of steamers in conjunction with sailing vessels, and the annexation of the island of Fernando Po to our foreign possessions. Simple and insignificant as the means may at first sight appear, they will be decisive in their consequences, and fully answer the end as far as the capture and destruction of slave-vessels are concerned. Steamers, it is obvious, will come up with these, at times and seasons, when our best sailing ships cannot touch them, and Fernando Po is a station, in the *sight of which eight-tenths* of the existing slaves must pass to be carried on. Commodore Bullen, whom you have quoted, says, " that if a look-out be kept from the shore of this bay, (in Fernando Po) scarcely a vessel could leave the Bonny, Calabars, Bimbia, and Camaroon rivers, without being observed time enough to signalize to any vessel lying in the bay to intercept her;" and he cites as an instance the capture of a slaver Le Daniel by his own vessel. This capture

* Papers relative to Sierra Leone, September, 1830, No. 57, p. 39.

was effected within four hours after first seeing her, although his vessel was then lying at anchor in the bay. Taking in these three happy circumstances together, the employment of steamers, the vicinity of Fernando Po to the coast, and that the island commands a sight of eight-tenths of the Slave Trade now carried on, I cannot doubt that *ten* vessels would be captured where *one* was taken before. I verily believe that our cruisers would make such havoc among the slave vessels in three months, that when the news of what they had done should reach Cuba, Brazil, &c., the insurance there would be raised to a frightful amount, and merchants begin to query, whether it would be advisable to send any more adventures to that part of the coast. So far for the first three months; but after this, other vessels would be on their way to the Niger, ignorant of what had happened, and would share the same fate. Here a fresh report of captures would be communicated to the people of Brazils, Cuba, &c., and what effect would this produce there? No insurance at any rate! No heart to venture again in this trade! And here I cannot help stating the benefit that Fernando Po would be to the slaves who should be captured on these occasions: instead of being carried to Sierra Leone, as heretofore, many of them in a diseased state, a voyage of five or six weeks, during which a prodigious loss of life has occurred, they would be landed there in health in three or four days, some of them in a few hours, where they would be liberated, and set to work, and earn their own main-tenance immediately. I have been writing hitherto under the supposition that we are at liberty to take vessels of this description bearing the Portuguese flag. It is said that a treaty is on foot for that purpose with Portugal, but if that should fail, existing treaties would bear us out in the cap-ture of such vessels.

But supposing these two measures should be successful,

as you think they would be, in putting an end to the Slave
Trade, what do you recommend next? You recommend
that a *new trade* should be proposed to the natives in
exchange for that of the Slave Trade, in the productions of
their soil; that is, by means of agriculture, by which their
wants, and more than their usual wants, would be supplied,
so that when the new trade should come fairly into play,
they would find, practically find, that it was more than a
compensation for the old; and that the rise of this new
trade should immediately follow the downfall of the Slave
Trade. But how is this new trade to be brought about?
You answer by *treaties* with the native chiefs; by *subsidies*
to some of them, which, though they would be important,
would be of trifling amount; by *purchasing land,* which,
though extensive, would be attended with little cost; by
introducing settlements among them, by which their industry would be directed to the proper objects of cultivation,
and that cultivation improved by our skill; by which their
youth would be educated, their manners and habits civilized, and the gospel be widely spread among them.

There is no doubt that if all these things could be accomplished, not only the Slave Trade would be abolished, but
the natives would never wish to return to it. Now you
have shown by historical proofs that *all these things have
been already done* in many instances in different parts of
Africa, and that the results have been highly favourable,
and this, without any particular pains being taken, except
at Sierra Leone; in fact, without any but ordinary stimulus
being given, the natives being left to their own will and
pleasure, and without any other incitement than the protection which a settlement in this vicinity afforded them,
and a simple declaration, " that they should be paid for
their labour." What would be the case then, were a great
company established in England, whose constant object

would be to excite their energies by the prospect of a suitable reward, and by instructing them how to earn it?

Let us now see what these historical proofs are (and I shall quote from them very briefly) on which you place so much reliance. Sierra Leone offers itself for consideration first. You say that " the accounts, soon after the settlement was formed there, stated that the natives crowded round the colony, both for education and for trade, and that the beneficial effect upon them in inducing them to quit slave trading, was *instantaneous*. That effect *has been continued*, and has *extended* in the neighbourhood of Sierra Leone to a very considerable distance round the colony. Traders bring down ivory, gold-dust, and palm oil as usual. Of late years a very *important branch has been added to the legal trade* for the cutting of timber for the British Navy, &c. &c.

The river Gambia presents itself next. " In the year 1814," says Mr. Bandinel, " a colony was formed at St. Mary's on this river. This colony has increased and flourished beyond all reasonable calculation, and is already *more powerful and wealthy* than any of those older settlements of the British in Africa, which were formed for the purpose of promoting the Slave Trade."—" The beneficial effects of this settlement at St. Mary's on all the tribes along the banks of the Gambia, are perhaps still more prominent than those which have taken place round Sierra Leone."

In the year 1833, a mission in connexion with the Wesleyan Society was established at Mac Carthy's island. " Before the abolition of the Slave Trade," says the Rev. Mr. Macbriar, " there were considerable factories here, but now that the slave market is abolished, and the natives can find a ready market for the produce of their lands by means of the British merchants, the *cultivation of the soil increases every year;* and the aborigines have been heard to say, that they now wish they had their slaves back again, because they could get more by their labour than they did by selling them to Europeans."

Let us add another of your proofs. The Rev. J. Morgan, to whom the Foulah mission in the same river partly owes its origin, recommends the purchase of tracts of land adjoining the principal rivers. He says, " that thousands would flee to such places of refuge as soon as they could be assured of protection, and thus a dense free population would soon spring up, and commerce would rapidly extend." I myself am connected by subscription with a settlement in this river, and the accounts from thence, which I see yearly, are full of the *anxious desire* manifested by the natives on the banks of it, to be under our protection, and to cultivate their lands in peace, and to be civilized and christianized.

We come now to the Gold Coast. In no part of Africa, says the Governor, M'Lean, was the Slave Trade more firmly rooted, or more systematically carried on than in these settlements." " But a great change has taken place since its abolition. The soil, which formerly did not yield sufficient for the sustenance of the inhabitants, *now affords to export* a very large amount of corn to *Madeira*," " besides *greatly increased quantities* of gold-dust and ivory." " The exports to Great Britain amount to £160,000 per annum." Formerly " the whole country was one scene of oppression, cruelty, and disorder, so that a trader dared not go twenty miles into the bush. At present our communication with the interior is as *free and safe* as between England and Scotland." Add to this the statement, that " several hundreds of the natives, through the labours of the Wesleyan missionaries, have embraced the truths of Christianity."

Having now made a few quotations from what you have advanced relative to our *own colonies* on the continent of Africa, let us quote from what you have said relative to other

parts of the same continent which are not in our possession.
The first of these which presents itself in the order of location upon that coast, is the country in the neighbourhood of
the Senegal. The natives having had reason to suppose
that it was the intention of the British Government, when
they took possession of this river, to abolish the Slave Trade
as far as their new dominions extended, were filled with joy.
" Seeing no probability of any further Slave Trade,'' says
Mr. Rendall, who was a resident of St. Louis, in the Senegal,
from 1813 to 1817, " they bethought themselves to *turn
their attention to agriculture,* and all *disposable tracts of
land* were in consequence *to be found in a state of cultivation.* The inhabitants passed from one village to another
without fear or *protective weapons,* and contentment seemed
to reign not only in the countenances, but in the humble huts
of the inhabitants." This account of Mr. Rendall is very
short. It is a pity that he did not dwell more largely, as he
might have done, on the *extraordinary industry,* which
this belief of the abolition excited; on the great quantity of
land put in cultivation for miles along the banks of the
Senegal, and on the markets which the people had opened
for themselves. I had an account of these particulars, as
they occurred, from persons at Fort St. Louis, myself, and
had occasion afterwards to transmit them to the Congress at
Aix-la-Chapelle, where I understood they were received and
read.

The next place in order of location is the Island of
Bulama, situated opposite to the country of Biafra, and not far
from the great rivers Rio Grande and Nunez. Here Captain Beaver, at the close of the last century, attempted to
form a colony. Two of the natives of the opposite continent
soon crossed over to him, and though he told them " *he
could have no dealing in slaves,*" yet their report induced
others to take *service with him,* and he never afterwards
wanted grumettas or labourers. In one year he employed

nearly two hundred of them. He never saw men work harder, more willingly, or regularly, generally speaking, than they did.   And what induced them, says Captain Beaver, to do so ?   " Their desire of European commodities in my possession, of which they knew they would have the value of one bar at the end of the week, or four at the end of a month.   Some of them remained at labour for months ere they left me.   Others, after having left me, returned. They knew that the labour was constant, but they also knew that their reward was certain."   To this account I may just add, that I knew Captain Beaver personally, and that I have heard these and other important statements from his own lips.   He was a captain in the royal navy ; and in private life he was most estimable, and a man of high moral character.

The last place in the same order, but some hundreds of miles further down the coast, which you quote, is the river Niger.   Unfortunately the gentlemen you mention have not been resident in the interior of this country, and therefore can only speak of what they saw and heard while navigating this immense river.   By this river, says Mr. Laird, one hundred millions of people would be brought into direct contact with the civilized world, new and boundless markets would be opened to our manufacturers, a continent teeming with inexhaustible fertility would yield her riches to our traders ; not merely a nation, but hundreds of nations, would be awakened from the lethargy of centuries, and become useful and active members of the great commonwealth of mankind."   And what says Mr. Lander of the disposition of this vast population of the countries through which this river goes ?   " The natives," he says, " only require to *know what is wanted from them,* and to be *shown what they will have in return,* and much produce that is now lost from neglect, will be returned to a considerable amount." But the most important evidence which you have cited for this part of the country is Colonel Nicholls. He tells us, that from his long experience in these and other parts of Africa, " there is one means, and he is persuaded but one effectual means, of destroying the Slave Trade, which is by introducing a liberal and well regulated system of commerce on the coast of Africa." He then gives us the substance of a conversation with one of the native chiefs on this subject, in which he convinced him of the folly of trading in the bodies of the inhabitants in comparison with trading in the productions of the soil, so that this chief gave up the Slave Trade : and says, " I feel convinced that I could *influence all the chiefs along the coast in the same manner :* but to be able to effect this, it would be necessary to have the means of moving with a degree of celerity that a steam-vessel alone would give us."—" Steam-boats would also be of incalculable use to commerce, by towing ships over bars and agitated currents, whilst, as a means of catching the Slave-ships, and protecting the coast from the depredations of their crews, *three steamers would effect more than the expensive squadron now maintained there.* I pledge myself to put an end to the whole of our expense, and *totally to suppress the Slave Trade,* in two years." O, how I wish that Colonel Nicholls could be sent again to Africa for this purpose! He is the only man alive to effect it. I know him well. His whole heart and soul are in the project. Besides, he has an intimate knowledge of these seas and harbours, of Fernando Po, and what it can do towards the abolition of the Slave Trade; of the mouth of the Niger, and the great rivers falling into it; of some of the native chiefs personally, and of the manners, customs, disposition, and temper in general of the inhabitants of these parts.

But why should I go further into "The Remedy" you propose? It would be a waste of words. It has already appeared probable, nay, more than probable, that if steamers were employed, and Fernando Po added to our possessions, the capture of the vessels concerned in the hateful traffic would be comparatively easy; that treaties might be made with the African chiefs, and several of them subsidized in our interest; and that the energies of the natives on that vast continent might be called forth in a *new trade*, in the productions of their soil, (which of itself would sap the foundation of the Slave Trade,) and that thousands and tens of thousands of these natives might be engaged in it. Again, you have projected a large commercial and agricultural company, which should take off their produce, and supply their wants. What can you *devise*, and what can you *desire* more, to put down the Slave Trade and to civilize Africa? I hope then that you will not be so diffident as you appear to be relative to the success of your measures : if they do not succeed, none will. I have studied the subject for more than half a century, and give it as my opinion that yours is the only plan that will answer. I cannot doubt that the Government would readily promote your views, if they were only persuaded that it was probable that the abolition of the Slave Trade would follow, and that a great part of the country, the moral and religious part of it, would be grateful, very grateful, to them for so doing. And now, my dear Friend, having read your little work twice over, and having formed my conclusions upon it, and finding these in unison with your own, I thought that you would be pleased with them; and thanking you, as every abolitionist must do, for the great labour you must have undergone in preparing your present plan, I remain, with great regard,

Your sincere and affectionate Friend,

THOMAS CLARKSON.

APPENDIX E.

Sir,

I mention how my time has been chiefly occupied as an apology for my abbreviated account of the matter you are inquiring about; however, thus much I can state and verify. When I was travelling between Der, the capital of Nubia and Epsambool, I met a slave ship descending the Nile, and as I wished to see what was going on in the vessel, I went on board to purchase some ostrich feathers. This was in March last, I cannot tell the exact date, as my journals are in Paris. There were probably 20 or 25 slaves, of ages between 10 and 16. There was one man about 30 chained to the bifurcated end of a long pole; his neck was enclosed by the two branches, and a chain from one end to the other secured him even from a movement of his head. The other end of the pole was locked to the floor of the hold of the vessel. It appears that this man had attempted to escape. I actually *saw* but this one vessel, but my interpreter told me that several slave vessels had passed us in the night.

I was in the slave market in Cairo; I saw many slaves, male and female, on sale; being an European, I was not permitted to see the white slaves, nor do I know that there were any on sale at that time. The black slaves I had free access to; and I was *told* that there were some white ones in the rooms.

I am, Sir, your obedient Servant,

WM. HYDE PEARSON.

APPENDIX F.

Copy of a Letter from the Right Honouroble Lord John Russell to the Lords Commissioners of Her Majesty's Treasury. (Laid on the table of the House of Commons, 8th February, 1840.)

Downing Street,

MY LORDS, 26th December, 1839.

THE state of the foreign Slave Trade has for some time past engaged much of the attention of Her Majesty's Confidential Advisers. In whatever light this traffic is viewed, it must be regarded as an evil of incalculable magnitude; the injuries it inflicts on the lawful commerce of this country, the constant expense incurred in the employment of ships of war for the suppression of it, and the annual sacrifice of so many valuable lives in this service, however deeply to be lamented, are not the most disastrous results of this system. The honour of the British Crown is compromised by the habitual evasion of the treaties subsisting between Her Majesty and foreign powers for the abolition of the Slave Trade, and the calamities which, in defiance of religion, humanity, and justice, are inflicted on a large proportion of the African continent, are such as cannot be contemplated without the deepest and most lively concern. The Houses of Lords and Commons have, in their addresses to the Crown, expressed, in the most energetic terms, the indignation with which Parliament regards the continuance of the trade in African slaves, and their anxious desire that every practicable method should be taken for the extinction of this great social evil.

T

To estimate the actual extent of the foreign Slave Trade, is, from the nature of the case, an attempt of extreme difficulty; nor can anything more than a general approximation to the truth be made. But after the most attentive examination which it has been in my power to make, of official documents, and especially of the correspondence communicated to Parliament from the department of Her Majesty's Principal Secretary of State for Foreign Affairs, I find it impossible to avoid the conclusion, that the average number of slaves introduced into foreign states or colonies in America and the West Indies, from the western coast of Africa, annually exceeds 100,000. In this estimate a very large deduction is made for the exaggerations which are more or less inseparable from all statements on a subject so well calculated to excite the feelings of every impartial and disinterested witness. But making this deduction, the number of slaves actually landed in the importing countries affords but a very imperfect indication of the real extent of the calamities which this traffic inflicts on its victims. No record exists of the multitudes who perish in the overland journey to the African coast, or in the passage across the Atlantic, or of the still greater number who fall a sacrifice to the warfare, pillage, and cruelties by which the Slave Trade is fed. Unhappily, however, no fact can be more certain, than that such an importation as I have mentioned, presupposes and involves a waste of human life, and a sum of human misery, proceeding from year to year, without respite or intermission, to such an extent as to render the subject the most painful of any which, in the survey of the condition of mankind, it is possible to contemplate.

The preceding statement unavoidably suggests the inquiry, why the costly efforts in which Great Britain has so long been engaged for repressing the foreign Slave Trade have proved thus ineffectual? Without pausing to enumerate the many concurrent causes of failure, it may be sufficient to say that such is the difference between the price at which a slave is bought on the coast of Africa and the price for which he is sold in Brazil or Cuba, that the importer receives back his purchase-money tenfold on the safe arrival of his vessel at the port of destination. It is more than probable that the general profits of the trade, if accurately calculated, would fall exceedingly below this estimate, as indeed it is certain that in many cases it is carried on at a ruinous loss. But your Lordships are well aware, how powerful and constant an impulse may be given to any species of illegal traffic, however hazardous, when they who engage in it are allured by the hope of very large and quick returns, if their good fortunes could enable them to escape the penalties of the law. It may therefore be readily understood how effective is such a stimulus, when, as in the case in question, the law itself is regarded with general disfavour in the society to which the violator of it belongs, and is reluctantly executed by the government of that society. We must add to this exciting motive the security which is derived from insurances, and insurance companies, which are carried on to a great extent, and combined powerful interests. Under such circumstances, to repress the foreign Slave Trade by a marine guard would scarcely be possible, if the whole British navy could be employed for that purpose. It is an evil which can never be adequately encountered by any system of mere prohibition and penalties.

Her Majesty's confidential advisers are therefore compelled to admit the conviction that it is indispensable to enter upon some new preventive system, calculated to arrest the foreign Slave Trade in its source, by counteracting the

principles by which it is now sustained.   Although it may
be impossible to check the cupidity of those who purchase
slaves for exportation from Africa, it may yet be possible to
force on those, by whom they are sold, the persuasion that
they are engaged in a traffic, opposed to their own interests
when correctly understood.

With this view it is proposed to establish new commercial relations with those African chiefs or powers within
whose dominions the internal Slave Trade of Africa is carried on, and the external Slave Trade supplied with its
victims.   To this end the Queen has directed Her Ministers, to negotiate conventions or agreements with those
chiefs and powers, the basis of which conventions would be,
first, the abandonment and absolute prohibition of the
Slave Trade; and, secondly, the admission for consumption
in this country, on favourable terms, of goods the produce
or manufacture of the territories subject to them.   Of those
chiefs, the most considerable rule over the countries adjacent to the Niger and its great tributary streams.   It is
therefore proposed to dispatch an expedition which would
ascend that river by steam-boats, as far as the points at
which it receives the confluence of some of the principal
rivers falling into it from the eastward.   At these, or at any
other stations which may be found more favourable for the
promotion of a legitimate commerce, it is proposed to establish British Factories, in the hope that the natives may be
taught that there are methods of employing the population
more profitable to those to whom they are subject, than that
of converting them into slaves, and selling them for exportation to the slave traders.

In this communication it would be out of place, and
indeed impracticable, to enter upon a full detail of the plan
itself; of the ulterior measures to which it may lead, or of
the reasons which induce Her Majesty's Government to

believe that it may eventually lead to the substitution of an innocent and profitable commerce, for that traffic by which the continent of Africa has so long been desolated. For my immediate purpose it will be sufficient to say, that having maturely weighed these questions, and with a full perception of the difficulties which may attend this undertaking, the Ministers of the Crown are yet convinced that it affords the best, if not the only prospect of accomplishing the great object so earnestly desired by the Queen, by her Parliament, and her people.

Having instituted a careful inquiry as to the best and most economical method of conducting the proposed expedition, I find from the enclosed communication from the Lords Commissioners of the Admiralty, that it will be necessary to build three iron steam-vessels for this service, and that the first cost of those vessels, including provisions and stores for six months, will amount to 35,000*l.* It further appears that the annual charge of paying and victualling the officers and men will be 10,546*l.* The salaries of the conductors of the expedition, and of their chaplain and surgeon, will probably amount to 4,000*l.* In addition to this expenditure, Presents must be purchased for the chiefs, and tents, mathematical instruments, with some other articles of a similar kind, will be indispensable for the use of the persons who are to be engaged in this service, when at a distance from their vessels. I have some time since given directions for the completion of this additional estimate, but with those directions it has not hitherto been found practicable to comply. The charge for this branch of the proposed service will not be very considerable.

I have to convey to your Lordships my recommendation that in the estimates to be laid before the House of Commons for the services of the year 1840, the sums be in-cluded which are necessary to provide for the expenses of the proposed expedition to the Niger, on the scale already mentioned, under the several heads of expenditure.

I have, &c.

(Signed)   J. RUSSELL.

For EU product safety concerns, contact us at Calle de José Abascal, 56–1°, 28003 Madrid, Spain or eugpsr@cambridge.org.

www.ingramcontent.com/pod-product-compliance
Ingram Content Group UK Ltd.
Pitfield, Milton Keynes, MK11 3LW, UK
UKHW010348140625
459647UK00010B/918